To Cyril Wolfe

Sincerest Best
Wishes
Louis Jannetta
15/04/07

King of the Maitre D's

Secrets of Almost Fifty Years Inside the Famous Imperial Room of the Fairmont Royal York Hotel

My Life Among the Stars

By Louis Jannetta

Rain Publishing Inc.

Burlington, Ontario Canada

ISBN 10: 1-897381-06-9

ISBN 13: 978-1-897381-06-9

Cover design and layout by Kara Elsberry

Printed and Bound in Canada

Publisher's Note

We invite you, the reader, to please take a moment after reading this novel to send us your feedback. Tell us what you liked about, or for that matter what you did not like about "My Life Among the Stars." Please send your comments to: comments@rainbooks.com or drop Louis a line or two directly: authors@rainbooks.com.

Disclaimer

Please be advised that while "My Life Among the Stars" has been written in a non-fiction format, the stories told within are that of the best recollections of the author. The contents within are of the opinion of said author, Louis Jannetta, and not necessarily that of Rain Publishing, Inc.

Table of Contents

Dedication and Special Acknowledgements

To my beautiful wife, Corinne, and our wonderful children: Patti and her husband, David; Frank and his wife, Teresa; Susan; Connie and her husband Pino Celebre.

To my grandchildren: Nadine, Michael, Paul, Frankie Jr; Michelle; Ashley and her husband, Kevin Pickett; Julianna, Joseph; and my great-grandson, Owen Pickett.

To my parents, Frank and Concetta Jannetta; my brother, John and his wife, Barbara Jannetta; my sister, Carmella, and her husband, Cesare Della Savia; and to my nieces and nephews, Anthony and Maria Jannetta; Peter and Annette Jannetta; Paula Jannetta; Mario and Leanne Della Savia; Maria and Tom Dykeman.

To my first cousins Louie and Angie Jannetta; Joey and Mariam Jannetta; Carmella; Pasquale, Gaetano and John Castrilli; Tony and Esterina Jannetta; Louie and Lucy Jannetta; Mario and Valerie Jannetta; Peter and Diane Jannetta; Giovaniana and Nicolo and Uncle Fiore Muccilli.

To my sister-in-law Connie and her husband Ron Harrison; my sister-in-law Georgina and Alex and their children, my nieces and nephews.

To my dear comrade of more than 35 years, Tony Bennett, for his generosity and treasured friendship.

To Vance Anderson, Tony's manager, who has always shown great generosity and has been there for me and my friends, no matter the situation. Thank you for your kindnesses and support.

To my dear friends, John and Kay Haunts, thank you for everything.

To all my comare and compare and their beautiful families. Thank you for blessing my life with your kindness and support. Frank and Tina Giannacci, Donnie and Rita Greco, Ralph and Josie Dilella, Arthur and Mary Dilella, Joe and Myrtle Soretti, Michael and Mary Leone, Jim and Adele Leone, Vince and Connie Pillo, John and Olga Mazzaccanno, Sam and Josie Demacio, Peter and Anita DeMacio, Fern and Jean Flaman, Paul and Gloria Iannuzzi, Arnold and Monique Iannuzzi, Peter and Stan Collini, Judge Walter and Helen Martin, Larry and Bernice Patrick, Lou and Wendy Myles, John Valentine, Pat and Wayne Anderson, Rosanne and Victor Deschenes, Paul and Gina Godfrey, Doug Drew and Zena Cheevers, Michael Simonetta, Bianca and Nanni Gerronazzi, Zoltan Szabo, Ralph and Rose Sazio, Domenic and Angie Virgilio, Earl Duffy, Lena and Angelo Vertolli, Fred Lawler; Lorenzo Grella, Mike and Jean DiBari, George Cross, Dave Perkins, Jerry Gladman, Rob Salem, Rita Zekas, George Anthony, Mel Walker, Bill and Patti Wagner, Mary Hislop, Neva Mariga, Ledo Monti, Irving Ungerman, Bobby Harriot, Gordon and Bay Cardy, Louise Pitre, Joan Mather, Jack Amell, General Rohmer, Paul Higgins, Bobby Orr, Daryl Sittler, Melanie Couts, Malka Patel, Irv Winston, Bobby Kutner, Mary Webster, Keith Bullen, Jim Woods, Mickey and Nancy Vetere, Richard Andrews, Gordie Tapp, Joe Boccia, Ted Nikolai, Harold Shipp, Les Salnick, Jim Glionna, Tom Sandler, Hugh and Debbie Shorthill, Lester and Mary Stanford, Ralph, Pat and Frank Ruffo, Dom Romeo, Tami Agboola, Michael, Victor and Frank Palermo, Alois Poltl, Tony Padalino,

Michael Mazza, Chris Layton, Eugene Boccia, Ron Lenyk, Jack Levenson, Ian Wilson, Tony Mainelli, Alice and Slim Allison, Joe Cardarelli, James and Dorrie Franceschini, Bruce Lloyd and Family, Vern Gazzola, Mark Gazzola, Michael Toth and Carlo Fidani.

The list continues on and on, for so many have touched my life and I wish to express thanks, but alas, my publisher would not let me print a hundred pages to do so. Know that you are in my heart and thanks always.

A special acknowledgement goes to:

All the waiters, waitresses, busboys, chefs, Maitre D's, and others in the hospitality and catering industries who give up so much to serve the public with professionalism, humor, and class, especially my staff at the Imperial Room. To my assistant of 25 years, Nick Anastasiadis, and Alan Chan who gave me so much support. And to all of my staff who sometimes worked 18 hours a day on all those sold-out days and holidays to make the room run properly.

And finally:

Zoltan Szabo. Zoltan has become one of the top sommeliers in Canada. I am very proud to say he started working for me as a dishwasher and did not know one word of English. Now he has become top in his career and I am very proud of his accomplishments.

Michael Simonetta. I will never forget your family's kindness when my family came to Canada from Italy in 1935. Thank you for opening your home and introducing me to the Columbus Boys' Club.

Tony Mainelli. Sundays will always remind me of you and your dear family, for in your home is where I spent so many Sundays. Thank you for opening your home to my mother, father, sister Carmella and me.

The Priolo Family. If it were not for you paying for the voyage from Italy to Canada for my father those many years ago, this story would not have begun.

Joe Cardarelli. I remember the many kindnesses you and your family showed our family when we arrived from Italy. Thank you.

To all of Corinne's and my dear friends for your love and support from the day I arrived from Italy in 1935 until today.

~Much love, Louis~

Fotografie

MARCA DA BOLLO
LIRE CINQUE

...lli Concetta.

MARCA DA BOLLO
CENT. CINQUANTA

MARCA DA BOLLO
CENT. CINQUANTA

(1) Spazio riservato alla fotografia della moglie

Firma del Titolare

Muccilli Concetta.

(2)

Autentificazione della firma di
Muccilli Concetta
di Giovanni
Il Podestà

Firma dell'Autorità

Dato 21 luglio 1935 XIII

(2) Firma della moglie

Chapter One
Roccamandolfi to Little Italy

I arrived in Toronto in 1935, in the depths of the Great Depression. I was seven years old and spoke not a word of English. My mother, sister, and I got off a train in the magnificent Union Station, hauling all our worldly possessions in luggage tied together with string. We were about to meet the father I had last seen when I was about one year old and only knew from a faded photograph mother always showed us to remind us that we even had a father.

The clearest memory I have of that meeting is of the uneasiness my sister and I felt as we saw our mother kissing this strange man and of how he knelt down to take us in his arms and kiss us too. A more vague memory is leaving the station and seeing the biggest building I'd ever seen right across Front Street. It wasn't the tallest building in Toronto. One building was a few stories higher. But this building, the Royal York Hotel, was not only tall, but stretched out along a whole city block. As things turned out, it was a building that would be my school and my home for most of my life, a stately, elegant place that was about as far removed from where I spent the first few years of life as anyone could imagine.

My family hailed from the region of Molise, a mountainous area in the center of Italy, about halfway between Naples and Rome, known for its beauty and a way of life that was unchanged for hundreds of years. In the center of Molise, at the border of the Matese mountains, lies Roccamandolfi, where I was born Luciano Michele Antonio Jannetta in 1928.

The landscape around Roccamandolfi features steep rock walls and green valleys. The ruins of an ancient castle built by the Lombards in 1196—Rocca Maginulfo—dominated the center of the town. Rocca was always a small town, a village really, with an economy based for centuries on the seasonal migrations of shepherds to the plains of the Capitanata. But between 1880 and 1920, more than two-thirds of the population left for various countries in the Americas, mainly the United States, Canada, Argentina, and Brazil. My grandparents were among them, and their son, my father, was born in Canada. But the family soon returned to Italy. I don't know what the population of Roccamandolfi was when I lived there as a child, but by the turn of the 21st century the number of inhabitants had climbed to 1,100. My father, Francesco, and mother, Concetta, moved into my grandparents' home soon after they were married. After my sister and I were born, father became ill and set off to Canada for an operation, saying he would send for us as soon as he could. We waited. The trip to Canada was paid for by my father's godparents, the Priolo family.

My grandfather, Giovanni, worked three small farms and looked after what passed for roads around Rocca. Like all houses in the area, our home was made of stone with three small bedrooms and a combined living room, dining room, and kitchen that was quite small, though it seemed huge to me at the time. It was big enough at least to accommodate the three of us, two grandparents, two aunts, and an uncle. Being stone, the place was cold and damp and my mother, sister, and I all slept in the same bed, partly due to lack of space, but mainly for warmth. Mother would always warm the bed with irons filled with hot coals from the fireplace.

It was a happy home and I led a happy life, though a hard one in many ways. I was only four or five when I started doing chores. We had goats, cows, pigs, chickens, rabbits, and a couple of donkeys to tend to. My mother and I would get up very early to collect wood, some to sell, some to use in the fireplace and stove. As I got stronger, I was assigned the task of fetching water from the piazza in the town. When it got dark, I grew scared and would bang the pails together to ward off any evil person or thing that might be waiting in the shadows. The fun came with daylight when I would be out in the fields with my young Uncle Fiore picking cherries, grapes, figs, and peaches or collecting nuts—walnuts, almonds, and filberts—to eat, sell, or barter. I liked stamping grapes with my bare feet then crawling underneath the vat just as the juice would start flowing, splashing my face as I tried to drink it.

Life wasn't all work, of course. The other kids and I would run around the steps cut into the side of the hill, climb trees, or ride horses and donkeys bareback. We'd play on the flat top of a gigantic boulder next to the church, pushing and shoving and teasing the girls. We threw buttons against a wall, with the closest button winning, a game that probably sparked the fire of gambling in my soul. A few of us more adventurous boys went into local caves with lighted sticks to stir up the bats and duck as they dived and swirled above our heads.

The church played a big part in my life, as it did for everyone else in Roccamandolfi. Our priest was shown great reverence. Everyone looked up to him and would genuflect and kiss his ring every time they met him. I liked going to church, especially to hear the beautiful music, and looked forward to the picnics we had after almost every Mass when the weather was good. The whole family would go down on the plain, with Rocca perched on its mountain before our eyes, and lay a blanket down on the grass so we could eat and talk and play under the sun.

I became an altar boy at age six, a great honor for my mother and great fun for me because I had the job of pulling the long rope that made the bells chime, calling the faithful to worship. I pulled the rope down to my feet and hung on for dear life as it pulled me up off the floor. It was scarier when I had to pull the rope while it was still dark and all the lights in the town were off. These early morning "chimings" were supposedly due to the war then going on in Ethiopia. A silly notion, but that's what we were told.

Best of all were the Christmas and Easter processions and the feast days. The first Sunday of June was the feast day of San Liberate, the most famous saint in our area. His bones and relics were in the parish Church of San Giacomo, as was a statue of him sculpted in the early seventeen hundreds by Paolo Saverio Di Zinno, one of the immortals in the history of the art of Molise and Southern Italy. The feast of the town's patron saint, San Giacomo, came on July 25. In August, there was a Feast of the Shepherd in the mountains of Campitello. All these festivals brought people to Roccamandolfi from miles around, walking or riding on horses and donkeys. This provided a good opportunity to make a few lire for the family by collecting grass from my grandfather's fields and selling it to the pilgrims to feed their animals.

There was an annual fair too at the bottom of the hill that attracted big crowds. In what was my introduction to the performing arts, traveling performers put on plays, mainly comedies, as everyone gathered around to watch. I didn't understand the plays, but I loved the sound of the laughter and applause and the look of the smiles on people's faces.

Then in the middle of July, 1935, my mother told us we had to pack. We were going on a journey to a faraway place called Canada to join our father. My sister and I were very excited, especially when mother told us the streets of Toronto would be lined with orange trees and we could pick as many as we wanted. Having never traveled very far from Rocca, and then only on horseback, we set out on a wonderful adventure that took just over two weeks and would carry us thousands of miles.

It began with a ride to Naples in a car owned by a family friend. Only officials or wealthy people had cars in those days, and my sister and I took great delight in waving to any children we passed on the road, as if we were some kind of royalty.

In Naples, we boarded a ship, The Roma, which took eleven days to sail out the Mediterranean and across the Atlantic Ocean to New York. Our accommodations weren't quite steerage, but close enough. We stayed in a tiny cabin with three-tiered bunks and day after day ate the grapes and rolls and nuts we'd brought with us from Roccamandolfi. I had the top bunk and, in the pitching sea, fell out one night and cracked my head open. The ship's surgeon stitched up the gash.

The immigration officials at Ellis Island had to work around the stitches as they shaved my head and dusted for lice. I didn't like that at all. I started thinking this new world might not be as pleasant as I was led to believe. After three days of processing, we were allowed to board an overnight train to Toronto where I finally met my father in the heat and smoke of the railway station.

My head was spinning as he took us to our new home. We shared a house with the Simonetta family on Gore Street near Clinton Street in Toronto's Little Italy. It was next door to the Lombardi's on Mansfield Ave., Johnny, who later went on to found "CHIN" radio, would baby-sit me and often woke up the neighborhood with the strains of his trumpet that floated down the street. His legacy lives on through his family Teresa, Donina and Lenny, who, I'm happy to say, are still very close to me.

After all the new experiences of traveling in a car, a ship, and a train the previous two weeks, I was faced with the bustle of a large city and a stream of people, my father's friends, who came to welcome us to Canada. That first night, my father shoved some food in my face. He said, "Manga la banana." I'd never seen a banana before. I hesitated, took a bite, then spit it out, saying, "Non, mi piace." (I don't like it.) His big hand struck me across my cheek. It stung and set the tone of the relationship I had with my father for the rest of my life. I ate the banana.

The next day he took me to a garage a few blocks away where he kept his horse and a wooden cart. I was excited when I saw the horse. I clambered up onto its back and promptly fell off. My father wasn't impressed. But I got into the cart with him as he made his rounds through Toronto's neighborhood streets, calling out in what was a surprisingly strong voice, "Banana ripe. Banana ripe."

Father may not have had a kindly spirit. In fact, he could be downright mean. But from those first few days I realized that he had something every Italian values above almost all else: a beautiful voice, untrained, but a fine tenor that could sing very melodic Italian songs. I soon learned he sang for many people at clubs and concerts and events of all kinds. No one had any money to pay him, but he always came home with cups and saucers and other gifts. He even performed on the radio -- Ken Sobel Amateur Hour -- in 1936. He might have won the competition too, but the winners were chosen according to how many listeners sent in oatmeal box tops. Italians didn't eat oatmeal. I never loved my father, but I respected him. He tried his best.

In September that year, I was sent to St. Francis School, my first formal education other than what was basically kindergarten in Rocca. I got to make some new friends like Mike Leone and Charlie Bagnato. They would take me by the hand and buy me candy at the grocery store run by Vincenzo and Maria Cappuccitti. Their daughter, Florence, and son, Mario, who was my age and in the same grade at St. Francis, worked in the store. The Cappuccittis were the most remarkable family in the neighborhood. They were wonderful to me and to my family. When I was eight years old, I'd deliver groceries for them with my little wagon. It wasn't just us who were so blessed. With very little money available during the Depression, the Cappuccittis kept the entire Italian community supplied with food, writing down debts in little black books, though never demanding that accounts be settled. I wish I had all the money that was never paid back. Sad to say, my good friend, Mario, died at a very young age, but Rocky and Gordie Cappuccitti followed in Vincenzo and Maria's footsteps and helped many people over the years.

At St. Francis, I soon learned what it meant to be an immigrant. It was a tough school in a tough neighborhood where a boy was expected either to become a priest or end up in jail. Most of the students were Italian and Canadian. A few had arrived from Italy not too long before I did. Except for one kid who called me Luciano, I was usually greeted with, "Hey, Wop-o." I was a wop; others were Italian. Quite a few of the boys at the school took advantage of me. They beat me up constantly. There were days when I had to climb a fence with barbed wire on top just to get out of the schoolyard. I couldn't believe this was happening to me.

Some of the toughest boys, especially one named Ernie, beat me up and ripped my clothes. Afraid to go home with torn pants and shirt, I'd go to Ernie's mother, a wonderful woman who was upset her son would do that to me, and she would sew my clothes so I could go home. Fortunately, I soon acquired a protector, Emilio "Buffy" Valentini, who was a few years older than me and would step in and lift the bullies off me. (When I was much older, he saw me fight Monte Bonomo in front of the Monarch Hotel and knew he didn't have to protect me anymore.)

Aside from the beatings, school was pretty much all right. I wasn't a great student but the school put on lots of plays and I discovered I loved to perform. The students at St. Francis were all Italian but the teachers were all Irish. So I found myself cast as Timothy O'Toole and learned to sing songs like the "Irish Carrie Dancers" and "Come Back to Erin." I had lots of incentives to participate. One year, a teacher who disliked me, accused me in front of everyone of stealing a quarter and, as punishment, wouldn't let me go bowling with my classmates. I went to the principal, Sister Odelias, and told her that if that was how I was going to be treated, I didn't want to be in that year's play.

She said, "If you're out of the play, we won't pass you." I did the play.

After a few years, even the beating situation got under control. Almost from the time I arrived in Canada, I began spending a lot of time at the Columbus Boys' Club, playing floor hockey, baseball, and football. I was 110 pounds, but chubby, and was never that great as an athlete, but I worked my heart out. Carmen Bush, who eventually was inducted into the Canadian Baseball Hall of Fame, organized our sports programs. A guy who trained at the Boys' Club and was quite a fighter, Frankie Pucci, was a couple of years older than I was. When I was about 12 and he was all of 14 or 15, we began talking about the great boxers of the era. He took me under his wing and taught me how to put up my dukes. I was able to get some punches in the next time a bully confronted me in the schoolyard. One after the other, the bullies got to know I wasn't a pushover. One after the other, they stopped fighting with me. It made for a much more pleasant school experience.

Meanwhile, I was always working on weekends, after school, and during the summers. I was always selling something. I kept selling bananas with my father for about a year after arriving in Toronto. Later, I sold newspapers with a friend, Nick Mainelli, from Little Italy, heading downtown to push our wares to people near the Eaton's and Simpson's department stores at Queen and Yonge Street. I sold fruits and vegetables in the summer and fish and chips in the winter. When I turned eleven, my father bought me a bicycle with a big carrier. I did deliveries for him for free and picked up nickels and dimes by delivering for other people, riding the bike up and down hills, carrying chickens, fish, apples, and bagels from Kensington Market. I delivered bread for the Health Bread Bakery where the trick was to get out of the bakery with the bread without paying for it in advance.

I also got a job cleaning up between shows at the Pylon Theatre. I started to see a lot of movies, both there and at the many other neighborhood theaters around at the time. At 12 or 13, with all the nickels and dimes I earned from my deliveries, I'd see three movies a day in the summer. Being at home wasn't all that pleasant, so I enjoyed being carried away into another world.

I grew to love the stars of the cinema. "Boys' Town" was one of the first movies I ever saw, and both Mickey Rooney and Spencer Tracey had a big effect on me, moving me to tears. When the earthquake started rumbling in Clark Gable's "San Francisco," I got so scared I ran out of the theater.

I liked cowboy movies with John Wayne, Hoot Gibson, Tom Mix, Roy Rogers, Randolph Scott, and, especially Hopalong Cassidy with his white hair, horse to match and black outfit. Errol Flynn was one of my favorites, along with Tyrone Power in "Jesse James." I also enjoyed gangster movies, especially with Jimmy Cagney and Edward G. Robinson. I especially loved musicals. I idolized Nelson Eddy and worked up what I thought was a great imitation of Al Jolson. I saw "The Firefly" with Jeanette MacDonald and the great Allan Jones several times, and loved Jones' big song from the picture, "Donkey Serenade."

All the faces on the big screen became an important part of my life. They had character and class and style and held out so many possibilities for a life more refined than anything I had ever known.

Two actors in particular always stood out. I enjoyed the accent of the great French lover, Charles Boyer, playing a Maitre D' in a film with Joan Fontaine. I used to imitate his voice to sound older and later, when I went out on dates, I'd try out some of his sayings and mannerisms to impress the girls.

The other was a character actor rather than a star, C. Aubrey Smith, who was Hollywood's favorite Englishman for decades. There was simply something about him that personified the British Empire and all that was genteel, courteous, and discreet. I was a bit too young to see him in classic movies from the early thirties like "The Lives of a Bengal Lancer," "The Crusades," "Clive of India," and "China Seas." But I caught up with him in terrific films like "The Garden of Allah" with Marlene Dietrich, "Little Lord Fauntleroy," "Wee Willie Winkie," "The Prisoner of Zenda," "Kidnapped," "The Four Feathers," "Waterloo Bridge," and so many others. He and other screen idols that I saw again and again not only entertained me, but let me live another life, at least for a while. They gave me something to think about and dream about as I rode my bicycle around town.

I may have been thinking about them as I rode out on missions for the nuns of St. Francis who often sent me down to the post office on Front Street to deliver or pick up mail. On each trip, I became more aware of the great building across the street from the post office, the Royal York, the largest hotel in the British Empire and the jewel in the crown of the legendary Canadian Pacific hotel chain.

When I graduated from grade eight at age fourteen, my family and I agreed it was time for me to get a job. My father approached Henry Capri, who came from the same area in Italy as my family, lived near us, and had become a figure of some prominence at the Royal York's restaurants which were known as the best in town. Father said, "Henry, would you please get my son a job." The hotel didn't hire people younger than sixteen, but it was 1942 and there was a war on. The supply of manpower wasn't what it was during the Depression. So I lied about my age, Henry winked at the fib, and I began a relationship with a great institution that lasted almost fifty years.

Columbus Boy's Club Band (Louis on cymbals)

Mama Concetta, Papa Francesco, Luciano, Carmella, and Giovanni

Chapter Two
A Talent for Service

In the late 19th century, the Canadian Pacific Railway became famous for bridging the Great Plains and extending the new country of Canada to the Pacific Ocean. In the last couple of decades of that century, the CPR made more of a mark by building some of the greatest hotels in the world -- The Banff Springs and Chateau Lake Louise in the Rockies, the Chateau Frontenac in Quebec City, the Empress in Vancouver, and several others. Oddly enough, Toronto was the last major Canadian city to have a CP railway hotel. But the company saved the best for the last. When it opened in 1929, the Royal York Hotel was the largest hotel in the British Empire — all 20 floors of it.

I had seen it from the outside from the moment I arrived in the city and many times since. But before getting a job there, I had never seen it from the inside. It was an awe-inspiring place. It had more than a thousand guest rooms, huge public rooms, a hospital, a library, a roof garden, and a concert hall. It had hand-painted ceilings, crystal chandeliers, and magnificent wall hangings. It set a completely new standard for opulence and hospitality for the city of Toronto, outdoing the Park Plaza and even the King Edward, the only other major hotels in town. Walking into it for the first time, it was certainly like nothing I had ever seen or experienced before.

When I started work as a busboy in 1942, I was assigned to the Venetian Room on the lower level of the hotel. It seated about 120 people at any one time, and during the months I was there, we'd have about 350 people for breakfast alone, most of them guests, but many who had traveled on overnight trains from Montreal or elsewhere and arrived at Union Station across the road early in the morning. I worked the lunch and dinner shifts too.

It was grueling work, but I was used to that. We opened at six in the morning, so I had to get out of bed at four to get to work by five and get into my white tunic and dark pants. There were linen tablecloths and serviettes, silverware, cups and saucers, and plates to lay out and other things to get organized. The main duty for the busboy was just to take the dirty dishes out and keep the sideboard clean, but if I had the time I could help out the serving staff a little, maybe getting part of the tip to supplement my $45-a-month salary. The Venetian Room had all waitresses at the time, and I came to admire them quite a bit. There were about six stations around the room, each with two or three waitresses. They worked so hard, carrying very heavy platters, always walking sideways between the tables. They had a long way to travel picking up bacon from the grill, then coming back to pick up omelets and other items along the way. They had to be very strong.

I was quite small and stumpy, a little clumsy, and not very strong at all. But I was diligent. I'd work at a furious speed, setting and clearing tables, running instead of walking, hurrying across the thick carpet in running shoes, which for some reason they allowed me to wear. It ruined my feet. I was almost crippled by the time I was 16, my arches had fallen so badly. I could barely walk then and I wear special shoes to this day.

The broadloom carpet in the Venetian Room caused me many problems. There was dancing in the room before the war and they used to pull up the rugs to provide a dance floor. So there were separations in the carpeting that attracted me like a magnet. I'd trip on the separations and the tray I was carrying would float through the air. It seemed like I dropped a tray just about every day I was there. The hostess, Mrs. Hutchison, tried to fire me more than a half dozen times, but she generally relented. What she actually did was ask me to resign, but I wouldn't leave. Her efforts caused me a lot of anxiety though.

On the good side, I had two of the most thrilling moments of my life up to that time while working in the room. The first was when Joe Louis, the Brown Bomber, the greatest heavyweight champion of the era, came in for breakfast. He was very quiet and very polite as I cleaned his table. I was pretty shy, so I didn't say a word and didn't know enough in those days to ask for an autograph. All I could do was look at him with the wide-eyed wonder of any fourteen-year-old boy in that situation. I felt an even bigger thrill when who should appear at one of my tables than the great C. Aubrey Smith himself, my all-time hero. He was in Toronto performing in a play at the Royal Alexandra Theatre. I was stunned to see him in the flesh. After seeing both those guys, I figured the Royal York was a pretty good place to work, despite the hard days, some of them more than 12 hours long.

It was also a good place to learn. I would watch the waitresses and observe their habits. The most memorable was a woman named Winnie who was a very good waitress. She worked so hard and truly set the standard for me. Some others might not smile, but Winnie was always warm and friendly, very polite, honest in serving her guests, and open about showing that she really enjoyed waiting on them. I learned from the guests too, watching people to see how they acted. I was still pretty rough around the edges, but I soon discovered that meeting some of the finest people in the world and seeing how they behaved rubs off on you.

I tried to improve my behavior, although it became very tough to make much of an impression on Mrs. Hutchinson. I'd always beat the other busboys into work to offset my flying trays. One time there was a big snowstorm and the streetcars weren't running, but rather than miss a day, I walked all the way to work through the drifts. It didn't win me any points. I couldn't satisfy her. Then one day I was the only busboy on my station for breakfast, so all I could do was carry out the dishes. I worked very hard but couldn't help out the waitresses in any way, so I didn't receive any gratuity from the ladies working there. No one gave me anything. In a fit of pique, I didn't come to work for the lunch crowd.

Mrs. Hutchison took me by the arm, dragged me up to the manager's office, and said, "This boy wants to resign." I was hurt and humiliated and indignant at her lack of appreciation for all my efforts. I wrote a letter to the assistant manager about what had happened, pouring out my indignation, just to get my sense of injustice down on paper. I'm not sure I mailed it, but if I did, I didn't get a reply.

After my humiliation, I walked over to the Imperial Room and asked for a job. Henri Capri again took me under his wing and introduced me as a busboy to the magnificence of the Imperial Room.

This was a new and glamorous world to me. I had had no experience of truly fine dining, and even breakfasts were elegant affairs then. The Imperial Room offered breakfast, lunch, dinner, and a supper dance seven days a week. It was a magnificent room with a staff of about 90, including 45 or 50 waiters. Behind the scenes were hundreds more workers -- the huge kitchen staff, of course, but also laundresses, glass men, experts in the silverware re-plating shop, and many more. Since most guests had breakfast in the Venetian Room, it wasn't unusual in the Imperial Room to have six or eight waiters to serve 12 guests.

My job as a busboy was simply to help the waiter, stocking up the sideboard for everything he needed to serve his customers, passing out rolls and butter, filling the water glasses, cleaning the tables of dishes, newspapers, and anything else left behind, carrying trays out and stacking them as straight as possible, separating the food from the silverware when there was time, and hoping the dishwashers would sort everything out when there wasn't. An awful lot of silverware came close to going out with the garbage. Two or three busboys were assigned to each station.

I was still a clumsy, fat kid, but I worked all shifts for a year and a half, rarely taking a day off, catching some sleep between the sheets in the laundry room or sometimes just crawling under a table in the back of the room between mealtimes to take a nap.

The head waiter, David Chiasco, didn't always like my sleeping habits, but he saw that I worked hard, that I liked people, and that people liked me. He thought I could be a waiter and gave me the opportunity to learn the ropes by waiting on assistant managers or other members of the hotel staff who came into the Imperial Room. If I made a mistake or made of a mess of things, at least it wouldn't be with a paying guest.

That wasn't always the case when I was a busboy. Barely 15 years old, I was cleaning off the table for Lou Chesler, who eventually founded the Seven Arts Production Company that took over Warner Brothers' films. But even in the forties, he was well known in Toronto as a stock promoter. I spilled a glass of water all over his table and nervously apologized again and again. Mr. Chesler leaned over and said, "My boy, you're going to be head waiter here one day." I am thankful he saw in me what I did not at the time.

At 16, I was promoted to waiter, a rare privilege for someone so young, especially in a place like the Imperial Room. But I was ambitious and a little more forward than others. I learned how to handle a heavy tray and how to serve a guest in a confident and friendly manner, always taking the orders properly, introducing myself, and being spotless at all times. I took care of my guests. I was taught to make them feel warm and at home.

Service was the big concern, service in every sense of the word. These were the glory days of fine dining. I learned what we called French service, although it was really Russian. With French service, food is brought on a rolling table to the guests. With Russian service, food is brought to a sideboard on a tray and a platter is brought to the table and the food is served with a spoon and fork. It was hard and heavy work.

If there was a party of ten, I'd often bring filet mignon and vegetables on a 24-inch platter with a 24-inch cover and ten large plates, then serve each individual—ladies first—the filet, then the vegetables all around, then the béarnaise or wine sauce, doing it all with as much grace as I could muster.

It was a very big room too, and waiters had to walk almost a quarter of a mile to fetch the desserts. Waiters also had to learn to deal with Ontario's restrictive liquor laws. We could serve beer and wine, but only if guests had something to eat. We kept pieces of cheese on hand to satisfy the requirement. We had to look away with some finesse if guests surreptitiously (and illegally) brought in their own liquor, which a great many of them did.

The customer was always supposed to be right, though I never really agreed. A couple who lived at the hotel came into my section one night and ordered Pacific Pilchard, a rather large sardine. I brought it to them on a silver platter and served it with a flourish in a beautiful presentation. The man said, "Hey, stupid, that's not Pacific Pilchard."

I said, "I beg your pardon, sir, but it is Pacific Pilchard."
"It's not. You're dumb. Take it away."
"Sir, this is definitely Pacific Pilchard."

"Listen, stupid..."

He didn't have time to get more of the sentence out. I threw the tray across the tablecloth, the sauce and greens flew into the air, and I simply walked away. David Chiasco backed me up and didn't discipline me in any way. There was never any call for a guest to berate a server that way.

But those kinds of people were the exception. I enjoyed almost everyone else. I liked being a waiter and looking after people, despite often getting home at two or three in the morning and getting up again at five to get to work on time.

The place was always busy during the war with soldiers, sailors, and airmen moving in and out of town, many of them training at the Canadian National Exhibition grounds along the lake not far from the hotel. Canadian officers such as General MacNaughton and Air Admiral Billy Bishop were frequent guests, as were many British officers. They were all very polite and articulate and presented themselves very well. British entertainers like Gracie Fields and George Formby came in when they came to Canada to visit the troops or help sell war bonds.

About 25 or 30 people lived in the hotel semi-permanently. Some were members of prominent European families who had come over to Canada to sit out the war. Alfred Dunhill, who was very nice, lived at the Royal York for some time. So did Sir Alfred Rothschild, a massive man who had eccentric eating habits. We had to seat him in splendid isolation. In the morning, he'd have grapes and spit the seeds on the floor. At night, he'd have lamb chops and toss the bones over his shoulder as if he were living in the time of Henry VIII. There were stockbrokers from New York who stayed for months at a time. Even more casual guests typically stayed more than a week in those days when travel was more leisurely. The staff could develop some good relationships, which were usually rewarded with pretty good tips.

As such a young waiter, I had to really work at making a mark. I thought I should sound older, so I'd try out my best Charles Boyer imitation to make a classy impression, going around to tables saying in a deep, seductive voice, "Good evening, Madame. May I take your order?"

In the late forties, the Royal Alexandra Theatre presented the play, "Don Juan in Hell." The stars were Charles Boyer, Charles Laughton, Sir Cedric Hardwick and Dame Judith Anderson, some of the greatest actors of the day. Naturally, they stayed at the Royal York and came to the Imperial Room for lunch. They were in town for two weeks, and I waited on them every day. I loved it, though I never tried out my Boyer dialect. I left them alone, of course, never asking for pictures or autographs or trying to engage them in conversation. Guests don't come to talk to waiters, and one of my skills as a waiter was knowing both where to be and where not to be. Besides, they were aristocratic, giving little thought or notice to the hired help. They had their own conversation going, and I was pleased just to serve them.

Other theater and Hollywood people, including some of my other idols, were more openly friendly and forthcoming. Edward G. Robinson called me Luciano and, much to my surprise, spoke to me in fluent Italian. My own command of the language had slipped a little. He was a very friendly sort no matter who was serving him. One day, I brought my lunch tray in to serve him and all the other waiters were crowding around his table. I said in a mildly threatening, theatrical way, "Get away, you guys, or I'll blow your brains out." Eddie laughed.

Later, another favorite tough guy, James Cagney, often came to town to attend the Royal Winter Fair, never registering at the hotel in his own name. I loved all his pictures. I knew the local couple who were acting as his host and hostess and who brought him to the Imperial Room a couple of times, always dressed in a black tuxedo. He was very cordial, a real gentleman who didn't mind a bit of conversation. Maurice Chevalier, on the other hand, didn't want to be bothered by anyone. Same with Henry Fonda, who kept very much to himself when he was appearing in a play some years later. I recognized that and saw to it that no one bothered him. He appreciated my attention and sent me a picture.

Everything was going along very well for me until Ontario liberalized its liquor laws after the war. The Imperial Room could now serve liquor as well as beer and wine with meals. Unfortunately, I couldn't serve liquor since I was only 19 and the drinking age was 21. So I was dispatched to room service for two years where no liquor was allowed.

I liked the new job. In fact, I grew to love it. Room service was a lot easier than waiting tables and serving from trays. Many guests would have standing breakfast orders from the night before and I didn't have to take their orders anyway. Pushing tables along the hotel corridors was very nice and a lot easier on my feet, which were always bothering me as a waiter. I didn't have to rush around. I could serve people in the quiet of their rooms, then relax on the floor or even fall asleep if I was tired, which I often was. I grew kind of lazy, and sometimes the managers had a hard time finding me.

There were always things that kept life interesting. Sometimes at the elevators, you could look across the courtyard from one section to another and see people in rooms, with their windows and curtain wide open, making love. Maids and bellmen loved to gather and stare.

That was always good for a few laughs, though I never dwelt on it. And you never knew who you'd see after knocking on a guest's door. One time I knocked and a huge guy opened the door. It was Anthony Quinn, another one of my favorite movie stars.

There were a few eccentric guests. A Mr. Maclean, who owned a bridge construction company, stayed at the hotel three or four days a week. He was known for going to Sunnybrook Hospital and giving money to all the soldiers recuperating from their war wounds. He also handed out money around the hotel, a hundred here, a hundred there. When he had dinner, the chef and room service manager would show up at his room personally, knowing they'd be rewarded for their attentiveness. Mr. Maclean would also sometimes visit the kitchen in his pajamas and throw money all over the place, whether onto the floor or into the soup. He didn't know what he was doing sometimes.

When it was my turn to wait on him, Mr. Headly, the room service head waiter, came along with me and said, "Mr. Maclean, this boy can sing."

"Really? Give us a song."

I knew three songs – "Santa Lucia," "Torna A Surriento," and "O Sole Mio." I didn't know all the words to any of them, but then, neither did they. So I made up my own words as I sang. When I was finished, Mr. Maclean said to one of his people, "Give him a hundred dollars." The person took me aside and gave me fifty dollars. I sang again and Mr. Maclean said, "Give him two hundred dollars." I got another fifty. By the time I finished satisfying his requests by repeating the same songs, I went downstairs with two hundred and fifty dollars which was great money in 1949 -- like receiving three thousand today.

Unfortunately, I threw it all away. One feature of staff life at the Royal York was never-ending gambling in the basement by the washroom. I had developed a fondness for gambling as a child in Italy, throwing buttons up against the wall. With all the crap games going on in back alleys in Toronto's Little Italy, the fondness turned into an addiction. I worked hard as a busboy and made some good tips. I kept money hidden under the linoleum in my bedroom and played games in the neighborhood alleyways all through the forties. But, sad to say, some people took advantage of me, throwing crooked dice.

At one stag party for a neighborhood friend, one man I admired tremendously, who was a champion fighter, threw crooked dice. I caught him with a third die, but he and another guy still muscled me and took most of my money. He went on to be a successful businessman, but I never had the same respect for him.

At the Royal York, kitchen staff, waiters, busboys, bellboys, page boys, and others had crap games going night and day. They were intense games, too. One busboy (who went on to have a very successful taxi business) used crooked dice. We almost killed him. When I was in room service, just about every trip to the washroom would cost me money, sometimes eighty dollars or, after my performance for Mr. Maclean, two hundred and fifty dollars. The personnel manager came down one night and was ready to fire me on the spot when he saw me shooting dice. But he didn't want to fire the guy I was playing with—they were both very English—so he couldn't fire me either. That fluke was all that kept me at the hotel. Eventually, the security staff stopped the crap games, but there were other card games going on all the time.The hotel looked down on gambling, though not always. A waiter in the Princess Lounge, Rocco, was a bookmaker. Everybody knew he always had lots of money in his pocket. One weekend in the late 1940's, a large number of Americans arrived at the hotel and exchanged huge sums of U.S. money for Canadian currency, so much so that the hotel's cashier had no money left to give people change. With the banks all closed for the weekend, management went to Rocco to help them out. He had five thousand and six hundred dollars, the equivalent of tens of thousands of dollars today, and gladly supplied the Royal York with the cash on credit so the hotel could still do business.

Another habit of room service and other staff was picking up a little extra to eat while going through the kitchen. A Greek waiter named Agapitos was one of the worst offenders. He could have been fired on many occasions for many reasons. He loved oysters and had a habit of getting a dozen oysters on a small platter and covering them with a big tray of other foods so he could carry them past the checker sitting on a high chair looking down. Many times, he would give the oyster chef a quarter to put a dozen oysters in a glass. He'd slip the glass in his jacket pocket to get past the checker that way. One day, he dropped a customer's bill and, when he reached down to pick it up, the oysters fell all over the floor. The head chef saw it and fired him on the spot.

The main-floor kitchen was for room service. The Venetian Room and the Imperial Room were huge, with a staff of about one hundred and twenty-five. It had pastry chefs, butchers, bakers, and all the rest. The Royal York prided itself on being able to make fifteen thousand dinner rolls a day, the best buns in the world -- very crispy outside and soft inside. With conventions and other events, it wasn't unusual for the hotel to prepare ten thousand meals a day. When I started, the soup chef prepared thirty-one different kinds of soup every day for lunch which the great chef, Henry O' Deau, tested by dipping his finger in each. In most places, diners were lucky to have a choice of two. With so much activity going on and so much food around, it was easy to sample a few things here and there. Everybody did it. I used to eat ice cream when nobody was looking. But the personnel manager came by one day and saw me eating a baked potato. My punishment was to leave room service and go back to the Imperial Room.

Agapitos almost got the boot one day when he was walking through the kitchen and saw a lady leaning over the chef's desk looking at some menus. Thinking it was Frieda, a cashier in the Imperial Room, he smacked her bum as he walked by and said, "Hiya, kid, how you doing?" It was the hotel general manager's wife (Frieda's sister, who looked a lot like her). She turned around and said, "How dare you?"

David Chiasco wanted me back in the dining room as soon as I turned twenty-one, but I didn't want to go. The personnel manager knew that. I still didn't want to go. I saw the Canadian Pacific doctor and told him how bad my feet were and pleaded to be kept on in room service. He recommended I look for another job, which stopped my complaining. So I went back to the Imperial Room. It was the best thing that ever happened to me, especially because I was starting to think about settling down.

A couple of years earlier, my chums and I would often go to the Palais Royale dance hall every Saturday night to dance and hear Bert Niosi's band. On one of the luckiest nights of my life, I saw a beautiful young girl, Corinne, and her sister, Connie. Being nineteen and shy and hating rejection, I didn't want to ask her to dance, but we did get to talking.One of my friends liked Corinne, so I went out with Connie a few times, but I was more interested in Corinne. I drove her home one night in my 1941 De Soto and phoned her a number of times, but I was turned away. It turned out her father, George, had fought in the war and didn't like Italians at all. About six months later, I saw Corinne down on the boardwalk by the lake, near the Club Top Hat. I approached her and we drove off to get a twelve-inch hotdog. We started seeing each other again. I was always busy, still working breakfast, lunch, and dinner, and was always tired. She started coming to the little house where I was still living with my mother, father, brother, and sister, and waited until I woke up. I was never much of a go-getter, even then. But I knew I loved her.

We got engaged and, in 1951, we were married. It was one of the first weddings in my little community that wasn't held in the usual Italian parish hall. We were married at the Prince George Hotel, in the Pyramid Room. It was a beautiful wedding despite the fact that, due to my gambling habit, I hardly had a dime to my name. My friends helped out. The hotel chef was Italian and lived across the road from me. The room's Maitre D' worked with me when I was a busboy. We had about two hundred and fifty guests at two-fifty a plate for a seven-course meal. Johnny Lindon, a boyhood chum and a great entertainer who replaced Moxie Whitney in the Imperial Room in the summers, provided a twelve-piece band, including himself, and didn't charge me a cent. I did a mean Jolson impersonation at the time, and I got down on my knees and sang to Corinne "You Made Me Love You." We left for a honeymoon in New York the same night. That started my life my with my wonderful wife, Patti was our first child, then Frankie and Susie came along, Connie our youngest, rounded out my beautiful family.

Life was good at home and at work as the fifties wore on. The Royal York, and especially the Imperial Room, became the place to have lunch for many of the most prominent and powerful individuals and families in Toronto. The same people would come every day. Many had their own tables. It was their home away from home where they could always get wonderful food and great service in an elegant and genteel atmosphere. From the 1940's all the way through to the sixties, the Toronto Trio—violin, viola, and cello—accompanied the meals. The trio had a different repertoire every day for both lunch and dinner. Some of the best string musicians in town played for our guests, including Murray Adaskin and John Adaskin, both famous in their day (and both of whom lived two doors up from me in the thirties when every house in my neighborhood that didn't have an Italian family had a Jewish family). Yehudi Menuhin used to come in many times for lunch just to listen to Murray and the trio play.

Over the years, I got to know all the prominent families of Toronto, like the Eatons—John David and the boys, John Craig, George, Frederick, and Thor—and the Bassetts—John, John Jr., and Doug. I knew moguls like Garfield Weston, Roy Thomson, Sam Bronfman, and Ted Rogers, stockbrokers like the Midlands and Walwyns, and the people who built much of Toronto, like the Brattys, Delzottos, and Tannenbaums. I knew Conrad Black and Izzy Sharpe, the founder of the Four Seasons Hotel chain, when they were kids. I knew Murray Koffler, creator of the Shoppers Drug Mart empire, when he had a drugstore at Brunswick and College. I had the pleasure of knowing four generations of the many families who kept coming back year after year.

I loved my job and I loved people and worked hard. David Chiasco suggested I take a night off to take my wife out. He said I could tell her I was going to be promoted to captain. I not only told her, I told everyone. But the supper dance head waiter didn't like me much and wasn't happy at all. He spoke to David, who then gave the position to someone else. I was crestfallen.

But eventually, at age twenty-five, I became a captain, supervising certain sections, helping waiters and adding an extra layer of personal service to the guests. Unfortunately, there was no money in the position, really, unless the guest showed his appreciation. Sometimes a waiter wouldn't give anything to the captain (a practice I changed when I became Maitre D' to make sure teams shared the gratuities because the captains did a lot of the work).

Everything went along nicely throughout the 1950's. The room was busy every night and the Palm Court next door was filled too. I was a popular supervisor. People wanted to be in my section. Service was service then and, with a staff of eighty-five, we'd often have two waiters and a captain for a table of two. Presentation was still everything, whether with the Crepes Suzettes or Chateaubriand, sliced at the table. We would de-bone chicken at the table or present a lobster, take the back off, serve half, and keep butter hot on the side.

We had special menus and hallowed traditions for many special days: St. Patrick's Day, Halloween, and New Year's. Christmas was the biggest day of the year, with a grand procession through the room. I spearheaded it for many years, ringing the bell, while the chef and the staff would parade a well-turned-out boar's head among the tables. Then we'd present a huge plum pudding, with the chef continuously pouring alcohol on it to keep the flame going during the march past. One year, as Chef Marcel Didier poured the alcohol, some fell on a regular guest and burned her shoulder. Another year, the alcohol also flowed a little too liberally and, while the guest was spared burning, the Chinchilla coat on the back of her chair wasn't so lucky.

Things started to change in the late fifties, however. The hotel was getting a little dowdy. Canadian Pacific Hotels decided to build an entirely new seventeen-story east wing, with all the conveniences modern travelers expected, and refurbished some of the older section. It was all done under the direction of the general manager, Angus MacKinnon, a wonderful and generous man who was expert at running huge organizations (he'd been in charge of catering for the Canadian Army during the war and had even written two textbooks on feeding mobile and static armies).

After nine years as a captain in the Imperial Room, I could sense that the people of Toronto and the kind of guests the Royal York was attracting were changing. The days of basically three hotels having a near monopoly were over. The Westbury Hotel and the Benevenuto had opened up. The economy was doing well, people were traveling, and young people were trying new things. They had much more broad-minded ideas about eating and drinking and having fun than they used to. A lot of our guests were moving around, trying different places, and there were a lot of new places to try. That was clear when one of our head waiters left us to run the new One-Two Club on Adelaide Street.

I went to the hotel management-Angus McKinnon and Chuck Buron, Food and Beverage Manager-and suggested we should have a little night club downstairs on the lower level where we'd had a lounge for years and years. They were receptive. Being new, Mr. Burton wanted to put his own stamp on the place. He liked my ideas and carried them through. As our meetings progressed, we refined the concept. Finally, at one critical meeting, with a wave of his hand across the table, he said I would be the new room's Maitre D'. It was a great honor, especially at the age of thirty-four.

Much as I loved the Imperial Room, being given the opportunity to run my own room was something very special.

In 1962, Mr Burton and Mr McKinnon decided to call it the Black Knight Room, a cozy space seating about one hundred and thirty people, with lots of high-backed chairs. The idea was that we would give the place a medieval feel, with the waitresses dressed as pages in the tradition of the days of the knights and the hostesses wearing high cone hats and flowing scarves. Our page girls wore red leotards and had short beige tops with hoods hanging down their backs. I wore my tails and white bow tie and vest.

The Black Knight Room was my baby, so I was very involved with all aspects of the planning and execution of the concept. It was a new and interesting experience. I worked with the food and beverage director, Frank Bilecki, and Executive Chef Marcel Didier, one of the best known and most respected cuisiniers in the country. We devised a very nice menu, with steaks and lobsters, lamb chops, Dover sole, and other wonderful dishes.

Then I started to hire and train the staff. I was a little unusual in that I didn't want to hire anyone who had worked in other restaurants. I wanted young ladies who looked lovely, had nice personalities, and could be trained to Royal York Hotel standards. We did everything first class. I thought we had the best standards in the restaurant business, and I wanted to instill them in my staff as they had been instilled in me over the years. I had to bring them along slowly. It took a while. Not long into the training period, Frank Bilecki came in and started to talk to them about wines and cuts of beef. I said, "Mr. Bilecki, I'm still trying to show them how to put on a tablecloth and set up tables. They're not ready to learn about wines."

The ladies were wonderful and, after about a month of training, we opened up the room. They made some mistakes here and there, and I let them make mistakes. I watched them serving people, then would take them aside and elaborate on the right ways and the wrong ways of doing things. After two months, they were dissecting lobsters, de-boning chickens, and making Crepes Suzettes.

I continually tried to get across to them that, this being the Royal York, certain proprieties had to be observed, not only with the guests, but with the hotel management and within our own team. One lady used to call me "dear." I explained to her that it was "Mr. Jannetta." They were very open to instruction, except for one young woman, an aspiring actress who was very emotional and a bit eccentric. Her underlying complaint was that she thought her outfit was demeaning. One day I had to say something to her about serving roast beef in the proper manner. She threw a tray at me and quit. (The next time I saw her was at the Follies Royale at the Chateau Champlain in Montreal during Expo '67; she was a topless dancer. But we had a nice chat then and got along well for years afterward.)

I told all of them how useful it was to watch people and see how they acted. Good people came to our restaurants, and class does rub off. I was quite proud that some of the Black Knight alumni

became very successful because they learned to communicate.
I always foresaw that the room would have to have live entertainment, starting with a nice trio so people could dance, then moving on to book local talent, mostly girl singers who performed very well. There were no great earth-shakers among them, although one, Gloria Loring, went on to have a pretty good career. Moxie Whitney did the booking, but this initial contact with managing stage acts deepened my understanding of the artistic world and what kind of handling was needed to keep performers happy.Right from the beginning, the Black Knight Room was a huge success. It was filled every night of the week. We had lots of people from Bay Street, Imperial Room regulars, and Hollywood actors and singers who were performing in town. I got to know Everett Sloane, one of the great actors in "Citizen Kane," very well. I had many conversations with Connie Francis and her father. And I struck up a friendship with Sal Mineo, then just coming off the height of his career after appearing in "Rebel Without a Cause" and "Exodus." The relationship continued whenever he was in town. (I last saw him just a couple of months before he was murdered in 1976.)

I found the whole experience of running a room energizing, even thrilling. It helped develop my understanding of people and staff and systems and helped me in my profession of respecting people and making them feel at home.

After a year, I was told that my old friend, David Chiasco, the Maitre D' of the Imperial Room was retiring after thirty years. Mr. MacKinnon and Mr. Burton decided that I should succeed him. I didn't know that I really wanted to go. I hated to leave the Black Knight Room. But the Imperial Room was the jewel in the crown of the greatest hotel in the country. I couldn't turn that kind of opportunity down.

Louis with his former staff at the Fairmont Royal York

The young ladies threw a going-away party for me and I introduced them to my successor. Ironically enough, it was Henry Capri, the man who had hired me as a fourteen-year-old busboy in 1942. I was happy that he would replace me. I wouldn't have felt right being his boss upstairs in the big room. (He was a great man who stayed at the Black Knight and became a local institution until he was seventy-six years old, at which point the place closed up.)

For me, this was the defining moment in my career. I moved upstairs and made a grand entrance as the entire staff in ranks assembled gave me a round of applause. Together, we began a new era for the Imperial Room and Toronto.

Champions

There had been a lot of boxing in the Italian district when I was growing up, with some really good fighters in the community. Guys like Steve Rocco, Frankie Branchetti, Baby Yack, and Frankie Pucci taught me how to defend myself against the St. Francis school bullies.

I became quite a fan of the pugilistic arts. When I was a kid, I'd often go to Maple Leaf Gardens to see local fighters such as Frank Branchetti and Arthur King and always followed the big names in boxing, which was why I was so thrilled to see Joe Louis in the Venetian Room in 1942. I never had any inclination to get into the ring myself, though I think I might have been able to hold my own.

I recall, at seventeen, finding myself in front of the Monarch Hotel after a baseball game. A few hundred people from various clubs were hanging around Mansfield Avenue and Henderson Street, just talking about the game. Monte Bonommo, who was coaching St. Agnes at the time, told me what a lousy second baseman I was. He wasn't really wrong. I was not that great. The only reason I was playing was that by working as a waiter at the Royal York I had gotten to know some people and was getting the sponsors who supported our Perkyville Club.
I was offended anyway, so I said, "Well, what about you? You're a lousy coach." Monte was about thirty-two years old, worked for a construction company, and was built like a pit-bull. He was also very well known and well liked, so a young punk like me saying such a thing to someone like him in front of his much older friends was quite an insult. I embarrassed him.

I turned and walked away, but he hit me in the face from behind, right in front of everyone. I was not one who ever wanted to fight, but we started into it. He hit me in the stomach, with a punch I can still feel to this day, and knocked me off the sidewalk. But with what I had learned and being in pretty good shape, I gave back as good as I got. I was very concerned about him landing a few blows on my face since I could hardly go into work with black eyes. I kept throwing my left, then throwing my right, again and again, and knocked him down a couple of times. Some other boys finally intervened and stopped the fight.

I didn't see Monte for a month. My next-door neighbor told me he wore dark glasses to work that whole time. Then I saw him walking along the street. I was never one to hold grudges and figured there must be a way to make up, so I went over to him and said, "Monte, if I made a mistake, I'm sorry." We shook hands and remained friends until the day he died. The apology marked the end of my boxing career.

But I kept the love of the sport and of its greatest champions. At twenty-five, when I was a captain, Jack Dempsey, the Manassa Mauler, came into the Imperial Room, though not to dine. He became a very successful restaurant owner in New York after he retired from the ring in 1940, and just wanted to look the place over. His big battles with Gene Tunney, including the famous "Battle of the Long Count," were before my time, but I recognized him immediately and went over to speak with him. A photographer who was there took a picture of us with Jack's fist on my jaw, but, being a real dumbbell at the time, I wouldn't give him the five dollars he wanted for the picture, so all I have is the memory.

I had better luck with George Chuvalo, one of the greatest of all Canadian fighters, who came to the Imperial Room several times. He came in with a promoter just before his legendary fight with Muhammad Ali at Maple Leaf Gardens in March 1966. Ali came in for dinner around the same time and said he'd knock Chuvalo out in five rounds. He put his hand up, showing five fingers, with me hovering in the background in my tails. The Gardens gave me five complimentary ringside seats to that fight where George proved Ali wrong, going the distance and showing the kind of talent and class that led Ali to say Chuvalo was the toughest opponent he ever faced.

Muhammad Ali

George Chuvalo

Steve Stavro, Anthony Jannetta, Louis & George Chuvalo

The champion I eventually had the closest relationship with was the one and only undefeated champion in any weight class in boxing history, the Brockton Blockbuster, Rocky Marciano. There weren't that many Italian fighters, especially ones who could knock out guys like Jersey Joe Walcott, Archie Moore, and even Joe Louis (well past Joe's prime, of course, in what proved to be his last fight). When Rocky retired, he had an unbelievable 49-0-0 record.

He was in Toronto in 1966 promoting the Chuvalo-Ali bout. I was hosting an Italian-Canadian Hockey League dinner in one of the Royal York ballrooms when a local hero, Vic Bagnato, a great fighter who was friends with Rocky, came to my event and told me Rocky was upstairs in a suite. I said, "Why don't you bring him down?"

Vic said, "He wants a hundred dollars."

I said, "What? This is Italian hockey and he's Italian." A hundred dollars was a hundred dollars.

Vic gave me the suite number, so I went up and knocked on the door. Rocky and I spent quite a while together. He still wouldn't come down to the dinner, but we had a great time talking about Italians and some of the fighters around the city, including Vic and his brothers. After that, every time he came to Toronto, and he came often, he would come to see me and we'd sit and talk in the Imperial Room for hours. He was a great athlete, one of the best. Getting to know Rocky as I did, I could agree with Jersey Joe Walcott's description of him: "He was a man of courage inside the ring. Outside, he was kind and gentle."

Hank Aaron

Dan Marino

A League of My Own

Of all the advantages and benefits I received from working at the Royal York, one of my most treasured was the opportunity to meet so many of my sports idols, especially hockey players. From 1942 to 1980, just about every hockey team that visited Toronto stayed at the hotel, and the Imperial Room was their dining room away from home. I met legends like Charlie and Lionel Conacher, King Clancy, Busher Jackson, Red Horner, and Eddie Shore, and, at about age 17, had the opportunity to skate with them at Varsity Arena at three o'clock in the morning. I skated and practiced with the Boston Bruins and scored three goals against "Sugar" Jim Henry who led the Bruins to the Stanley Cup finals in 1953. I became good friends with Conn Smythe, the mastermind of the Toronto Maple Leafs and the builder of Maple Leaf Gardens. Conn celebrated his birthday in the Imperial Room every year until his death. I got to know Jean Bellevaeu, Maurice Richard, Henri Richard, Bobby Hull, Gordie Howe, Stan Mikita, Joe Primeau, Phil Esposito, Wayne Gretzky, and so many others.

Bobby Hull

Maurice Richard & Alan Stanley

This meant so much to me because I've loved hockey since I arrived in Canada and wanted to play the game just like other Canadian kids. Hockey is the Canadian way of life. But my family didn't have much in the mid-thirties. I was too busy helping my dad to have time for hockey and we couldn't afford skates anyway. Even when things improved a little bit, my parents would never buy me a pair of skates. They were old-fashioned and were afraid I would fall and break a leg. It wasn't until I was thirteen that I finally got a pair and started playing. I was never that great. I could stickhandle and was a dedicated competitor, but was never much of a skater.

Wayne Gretzky, Phil Esposito, & Robert Martella

Jean Bellevaeu and John Jannetta

Marcelle Pronovost, Gordie Howe, Louis, Jim Morrison, Terry Sawchuck

Steve Stavro with Louis

Eventually, I became good enough—at least in my own mind—to play in an organized league. All the time I was working at the Royal York in the 1940's I'd often get up at four in the morning to get to a game at rinks in places like Nobleton and Markham. Sometimes I'd stay out until midnight with some Toronto team or other, waiting for a little ice time. Most of the time, I'd end up just sitting on the bench for 60 minutes. I spent most of my time on the bench even in practice. It was frustrating.

Louis

Finally, I figured, 'Enough of this nonsense.' There was only one thing to do. At seventeen, three years after I began working at the Royal York, I started my own league, with two teams and such small rosters that the coach had to use me. I became the first hockey player who was also a league founder and president.

Italian Hockey League

It wasn't an entirely self-serving decision. When I got here from Italy, we had nothing and Canada took us in. Canada gave us food when we were hungry and warm clothes when we didn't have any. This was the only way I knew how to repay the debt. I formed what eventually became the Canadian Italian Hockey League as a way to give the fellows who grew up in my neighborhood something we could do together as we got older. Later, we also wanted to help keep young Italian kids off the streets and give them an incentive to behave.

I started small in 1946, rounding up enough young Italian boys to make two teams, collecting their money for ice time in the middle of the night at Ravina Gardens. We played a game a week. I had one firm rule. No one would sit on the bench. Everybody would get ice time. I only allowed eleven players on each team, so we all had to work hard. At first, we didn't even have any sweaters, but nobody minded because we all got the chance to play. The next year, I found sponsors to buy sweaters, got two more teams and officially formed the league.

Over the years, the Canadian Italian Hockey League became the largest ethnic hockey organization in the country. It gave players of all degrees of skill a chance to fulfill their dreams. We never cared how good a hockey player was. If he came out for the team, he could play for as long as he wanted. That was the rule. But we were good enough that, in the 1950's, I also formed an all-star squad to play exhibition games and charity events to raise money for worthy causes. I played myself for many years, even leading the league in scoring one year. But I stopped in 1963, partly because running the league was taking up so much time, partly because my heart went out of the on-ice game when Toronto's popular mayor, Don Summerville, died of a heart attack while playing goal in a charity game the league had organized.
Through the CIHL and the Royal York, I developed close friendships with many of the great stars from all teams in several eras. Many supported the league as guest referees or in other capacities, giving generously of their time and talents. While I rooted for the Leafs, of course, I never tried to play favorites. I wanted to be everybody's friend.

One of my closest friends, at least for a time, was Terry Sawchuck, the great goalie who played for Toronto in the mid-sixties. Terry was a fierce competitor, and during a game between the Leafs and the Montreal Canadians, I wished members of both teams good luck as they went out onto the ice. Why not? I had friends on both teams. No other Leaf seemed to mind, but Terry took great offense. I thought the whole incident was insignificant, but Terry felt betrayed. I tried to apologize for any offense, but he said, "Don't give me that bullshit. I saw you wishing them good luck. You lost a friend."

Terry Sawchuck

I couldn't really understand his attitude. I told the story to the Leaf stalwarts, Punch Imlach and King Clancey. They said, "You can't sit on the fence." The next year when Terry was back with the Detroit Red Wings, I teamed up with Gordie Howe to approach Terry and at least say hi. Terry told me to go f… myself. After he'd been traded to the New York Rangers, he and his teammate, Ron Stewart, were lunching together in the Imperial Room. When he saw me, Ron waved and smiled. I went over to their table and said, "Hi, Ron." Terry got up and walked out of the room. **One of my biggest regrets is that Terry died the following summer without ever speaking to me again.**

My other hockey memories, with both the pros and my own guys, are much happier. Most of my dreams for the league came true, though not all. I used to dream that we'd develop talent for the majors, and I tried expansion. It never worked. But we did have some distinguished graduates. Gino Cavellini played with us a few years and went on to play in the National Hockey League with the St. Louis Blues. Gus Badali played with us and became an agent for a lot of top pros, including a skinny seventeen-year-old kid, Wayne Gretzky, who Gus guided to the Edmonton Oilers. John D'Amico got his start with us as a referee before becoming one of the NHL's most respected linesmen.

Phil Esposito, Louis, John Aird, & Wayne Gretzky

FRANK LENNON/TORONTO S

Honoring Jannetta: Ex-hockey great Phil Esposito, left, and Edmonton Oilers' Wayne Gretzky, right, joined Lieutenant-Governor John Aird in honoring Louis Jannetta, second from left, for his work in founding t Canadian Italian Hockey League. The appreciati night was held at the Royal York Hotel.

Hockey league founder feted

Toronto Star, August 27,1982 Photo by Frank Lennon/Toronto Star Reporter Frank Orr/Toronto Star

Fern Flaman

Former Montreal Canadian Hockey Greats

Yvan Cournoyer and Jacques Laperriere with Louis

Cam Neely

Most of all, I had a dream of some day bringing a hockey team of players with Italian backgrounds back to my homeland. I almost accepted that it was just a pipe dream, but after the league grew and I put together the all-star squad to compete in charity matches, I decided the all-star team would be the means to get us overseas.

I went to Italy to make arrangements, meeting with the president of the Federation of Italian Sports on Ice. We arranged a 12-game tour for 1963, playing town and college teams for two games each in Milan, Bolzano, Turin, Genoa, and Cortina, plus two more in Switzerland.

My home village between Rome and Naples was well below the Italian hockey belt, which pretty much stopped at Genoa in those days. After people started seeing so much hockey on television during the Olympics and the World Championships, interest in hockey became quite high in northern Italy. I was looking forward to showing them a little North American-style body checking.

Things got very exciting. Most of the players would be our league's all-stars, but we hoped to fill out the squad with Italian-Canadian players who used to be professionals but had regained their amateur cards or advanced players who played at least some senior-level hockey.

I enlisted some old pros I had come to know. The first player signed up for the tour was an old friend, Pete Babando. Pete broke in with Boston in 1947-48 with 23 goals, played in Chicago and New York, and was a Detroit Red Wings star in the 1950 Stanley Cup playoffs. He was the hero in that series when he scored the Cup-winning goal in the third overtime period of the seventh game. At 38, he was still playing in the Eastern Hockey League and I had him scout the amateur circuits he'd been playing in for several years. Lou Fontinato, who used to play for the Canadians and the Rangers, became my coach. He was a popular choice. "Leaping Lou" was a favorite around the NHL for nine years until a neck injury forced him out of the game.

We raised money for three years. I hounded merchants, leaned on some of my NHL friends, convinced the Italian federation to pay our expenses once we reached Italy, and tried to arrange a deal with Alitalia to get us there. My fundraising efforts were helped out by a letter I received in 1962 from another contact I'd made at the Royal York:

VIVA JANNETTA!

The team that won the 1962-63 title in Jannetta's Canadian-Italian Amateur Hockey League.

A SELF-ADMITTED "PIPE DREAM" born 11 years ago, is going to come true for Toronto's Lou Jannetta come late March of 1965.

The hockey fan on the street may never have heard of Lou Jannetta but he's a big man in the sport. He never played professionally and doesn't have a part in the sprawling National Hockey League chains that cover Canada and the United States. But without the Lou Jannettas, the sport would lose much of its reason for being so popular. And that's why everyone is glad to see Lou Jannetta's dream come true.

Jannetta, you see, was born in Italy and was brought to Toronto when he was seven years old. He never put on a pair of skates until he was 18 but learned hockey well enough to play in the Toronto Hockey League and 11 years ago he formed the Canadian-Italian Hockey League in that city.

That must have been when the dream first came to Lou Jannetta, the idea of some day bringing a hockey team comprised of players with Italian backgrounds back to his homeland. Some five years ago the league had grown from two to four teams and Lou put together an all-star squad to compete in charity matches whenever the need arose. This was in addition to the regular Thursday night doublehead-

(Continued on page 8)

6

CANADA

PRIME MINISTER - PREMIER MINISTRE

Mr. Louis Jannetta,
117 Silverhill Drive,
Islington, Ontario.

Dear Mr. Jannetta:

It is my pleasure to extend to the Canadian Italian Amateur Hockey League my congratulations for the efforts put forward by its leaders in sponsoring and promoting amateur competition.

The physical well-being of young Canadians will benefit greatly through participation in amateur sports, and your efforts in this connection deserve high commendation.

Prime Minister.

OTTAWA,
1962.

It took an awful lot of work, but after a couple of years, we finally had everything in place. Then, two weeks before we were to leave, the Canadian Amateur Hockey Association told us we couldn't go. We didn't have CAHA sanction. My contacts got the word out that this was a blow, not only against us, but against Italy. The mayor of Toronto and the premier of Ontario backed us up and complained, though it took higher authority to get things back on track. The new recently-elected Prime Minister Lester Pearson sent a message to the association: "I naturally regret anything that might stand in the way of the already warm ties between Canada and Italy." The CAHA backed off.

It was a wonderful tour. It meant a great deal to some of the kids to go to Italy and play in front of their grandparents and old family friends. We all attended Mass at St. Peter's and heard His Holiness Pope Paul VI give us his blessings. Through the good offices of one of our supporters, Helen Krug, my brother, John, Toronto Alderman Joe Piccinninni, and I were even granted a private audience with the Pope, which for me was the thrill of a lifetime. After I was introduced to him as the league president, I presented him with one of our pucks. He thanked me for the puck and wished us good luck for the rest of the tournament. The team went through its games undefeated and received good attention in the Italian press.

Pope Paul VI, Louis, John Jannetta and Judge Joseph Piccinninni

We were invited back in 1972. That trip wasn't as happy, though we still had a great deal of fun. Our guys played a bit rougher than they were accustomed to over there. At our last game in Bolzano, the official asked me to make our boys take it easy. I passed the message on to Lou Fontinato, who just shot me a look and told me that he was the coach (which ended Lou's coaching of the Italian All-Stars). What a night. Fans were throwing stuff at me in the stands. Maybe that's why we were never invited back.

My next big dream for the league came true around 1980. I was watching Sunday morning television on Toronto's multicultural channel, CFMT-TV, and had an inspiration. I called the station manager and said, "With all due respect to the cloth, but you have a priest, a rabbi, some old cartoons, and Johnny Lombardi trying to talk Italian on there. Why not show the Canadian Italian Amateur Hockey League games?"

The station showed interest, so I revamped the league. I named six teams after Italian provinces—Abruzzi, Puglia, Calabria, Sicilia, Friuli, Lazio—and put ads in Italian-language newspapers inviting prospects to try out. We were flooded with applications, over 500 players for the six teams. Eventually, our games were broadcast live in prime time on the Toronto channel and tapes of the games were shown in Italy on two stations in Rome and one in Friuli.

Through the years, many stars put their names and money behind the little league that grew, contributing equipment and attending fund-raising banquets and other events I organized. And not only NHL stars. Vaughn Monroe came to the arena to drop the opening puck at an early-morning game. Tony Bennett dropped the puck a number of times and one year presented the CIHL's Most Valuable Player award. The level of support was heart-warming to me.

One of my greatest pleasures came at the annual fund-raising dinner in the mid eighties. I filled the Canadian Room at the Royal York with 800 people at $200 a ticket, with Wayne Gretzky and Phil Esposito as head table guests. All of the money raised went to Villa Columbo, the Italian old-aged home. I took it as a measure of how far the league had come when Wayne told the audience, "Louis and I were in the Vatican in Rome when all of a sudden he disappeared. I looked up and there he was on the balcony with the Pope. People in the crowd started to ask, 'Who's that guy in the white cap up there with Louis?'

Brad Diamond, Tony Bennett, Louis and Judge Joseph Piccinninni

Chapter Three
Creating a Showcase

Much as I loved becoming Maitre D' of the Imperial Room, I often felt like I was in some sort of time warp. Except for an occasional fresh coat of paint, the room had barely changed since the hotel had opened in 1929. It was still open for breakfast, lunch, and dinner seven days a week. Dinners were still leisurely affairs, lasting most of the night. Guests still danced between courses, as they did in earlier decades to Horace Lapp or Mart Kenney and his Western Gentlemen or to Moxie Whitney, a very popular bandleader who was still there when I took over the room. But attendance kept falling. Some nights there were only a hundred people there, many of whom I'd known since the 1940's. It was an "old Toronto" audience, happy with their roast beef and a turn or two on the dance floor.

It wasn't long before I started to agitate for change. Things were transforming in the city in the early sixties. It was growing rapidly and, with all the immigrants flooding into it in the post-war years, especially from Europe, Toronto was becoming a lot more sophisticated. Many fine gourmet restaurants and new hotels and night spots were opening up. There were new cabarets. The Yorkville section of town was starting to attract people who wanted more than a Flaming Steak Diane and a foxtrot and a waltz. They wanted a show. More and more people wanted a memorable night out, and there was an awful lot of competition for their business. It was very clear to me that we had to do something different if we were going to even survive, let alone get the Imperial Room back at the top of the list of places to go. Otherwise, we'd be a victim of the changing times and changing public tastes.

I suggested to the hotel general manager, Angus McKinnon, and the manager, Pat Fitt, that we start bringing in name entertainers, signing the best nightclub acts available. The only other hotels in the city that had previously done so, the Barclay, which had presented entertainers such as Joe E. Louis and Sammy Davis, and the Prince George, where Lena Horne appeared, had closed or changed their policy. If we started booking name acts, we'd be the only game in town. I reminded him that the entertainment policy at the Black Knight Room, even with local talent, had filled the place every night of the week and that, as Maitre D' of the Imperial Room, I should know what was right for the room. In such a classy and venerable establishment, we needed to do something on a much grander scale than we did in the Black Knight. I fought long and hard to bring in big acts. Mr. McKinnon thought I was bothering him too much. It took six months and meeting after meeting after meeting, but he eventually listened and the decision was taken.

We tested out a new policy by booking Nelson Eddy for a New Year's engagement. He was a safe bet. Our regular audience was almost guaranteed to look on him favorably. The response vindicated my position to the management. We were booked three weeks in advance. After that, we booked him for a longer run.

Having Nelson there gave us the profile we needed to stand out from the competition. It also marked the beginning of a new stage in my long romance with the stars. I idolized Nelson Eddy and saw almost all his movies. I was a little too young to see his first collaboration with Jeanette MacDonald, "Naughty Marietta," but I think I saw all the other seven movies that "America's Singing

Nelson Eddy

Sweethearts" made together. They were great. He was good on his own too with a beautiful baritone voice that I loved listening to. He so obviously loved singing.

On the silver screen, Nelson was dashing and sincere and could bring people to tears when he sang. On radio, he was thrilling to hear.

When his film career was over, he tried television but never really made it on the new medium, so he spent the rest of his life singing in night clubs. His act became famous in the fifties when he started working with Gale Sherwood, a singer from Hamilton, Ontario, who sang and toured with him for many years.

He sold out weeks in advance, two shows a night. The only thing that disappointed me was that he'd sing all these great songs from opera and operetta, then suddenly sing a country and western song and do a jig on stage. As great as he was, there were some songs where people hardly applauded, even for Victor Herbert's "Ah, Sweet Mystery of Life." I'd be at the side of the stage getting the audience going.

Off stage, I found him to be a gracious, humble, even shy man who was very easy to get along with and delightful company over a lunch or dinner. He and Gale were always together. He wouldn't even get a haircut without her being there to oversee the procedure. They'd often come down in the afternoon, checking that everything was okay with the stage and the sound system. When he came in, I'd break out in a song from one of his movies or an Italian favorite. I couldn't help myself. "Rosemarie" or "O Sole Mio" would just pour out of me. On his last night, he said in his deep baritone voice, "Louis, come up here. Give us a song."

I was smart enough not to. It wasn't that I was shy. I'd been on stage in a couple of shows in Toronto. I just went up and said, "Under any other circumstances, I'd be happy to sing. But with you here beside me, I'm not that much of a fool. But I thank you for the invitation, and I thank you for being here with us. You're phenomenal. And you're my hero." Then, as always, I led the applause.

He did such good business we would have had him back many more times. But sadly, Nelson had a cerebral hemorrhage on stage in Palm Beach, Florida, during one of his shows with Gale and died a few hours later -- far too young.

But with the new policy we inaugurated with Nelson, the Imperial Room never looked back. At the time, I didn't know enough about the various acts that were available. I didn't have the qualifications. So Moxie Whitney, our orchestra leader who had some expertise in the field, began booking the entertainment.

I can't deny there was some resistance from our regular audience when we started doing shows. Some of our guests weren't interested. They still wanted to come for dinner and stay all night for the dinner dance. Personally, I thought dancing was very popular on Friday and Saturday nights only; entertainment filled up the room every night. Most times two shows a night were filled. It took a while to educate them. Many complained when I began putting tables on the huge dance floor. I asked, "Do you want dances or artists? You can't have both."

The Imperial Room wasn't built as a nightclub. The tables were up and along the sides of the room behind a rail. The center of the room was a sunken well for a polished dance floor that extended from the very small stage at the north end where the band played all the way back to the south wall of the hotel. I realized that the room was too large and impersonal to do justice to the act or the audience, which is why I started placing extra tables on the floor, coming closer and closer to the stage. We were experimenting.

The stars themselves proved to be our best tutors. They taught us how to make the room more sophisticated. After all, we were new in the business and they'd already been there and back. My education started with one of our earliest acts.

Jane Morgan, a beautiful blonde and talented singer, was a pretty popular performer on radio. She was a Julliard graduate who found it tough going in the States in the early fifties, so she went overseas and became the toast of Europe. She sang in just about every major club. So she knew what was what. When she returned to America, she had a couple of hit songs, especially "Fascination," which really made her career.

When she came to the Imperial Room, she found its atmosphere too cold and uninviting. She suggested reducing the size of the dance floor to make entertainers feel more in touch with the audience and give the room a warmer atmosphere. In the meantime, she serenaded our guests by getting off the stage and wandering from table to table on the rails with a hand microphone.

The singer and pianist Hildegarde, or "The Incomparable Hildegarde" as she was known, had much the same opinion of the room. She didn't want to be on the stage either and she was pretty blunt about rearranging things to build some rapport with her audience.

Because of her hit songs of the thirties and forties like "Darling," "Je Vous Aime Beaucoup," "The Last Time I Saw Paris," and "I'll Be Seeing You," many people thought Hildegarde was some sort of continental chanteuse. But she was just a Wisconsin farm girl, a classically-trained pianist who worked in silent movie houses and vaudeville before becoming "The First Lady of Supper Clubs," as Eleanor Roosevelt called her. She insisted that her piano be in the middle of the bare dance floor. There she sat, with her trademark white opera gloves and lace handkerchief, handing out long-stemmed roses to the audience.

One day as I was moving some tables onto the floor to fill in the seating around Hildegarde's piano, Angus McKinnon, the general manager, walked in, took a look at what I was doing, and said, "Louis, don't be so greedy!"

I said, "It's not a matter of greed, Mr. McKinnon. It's about making an atmosphere where the artist can communicate. It's about intimacy. People want this. They wouldn't be here if they didn't want to see the show. And we have to create an atmosphere. We have to have the artists up close to the audience in a big room like this."

I couldn't seem to make my point clear until we booked the great Sophie Tucker, one of the most popular American entertainers of the first third of the century. There was a trooper, "The Last of the Red Hot Mamas." Sophie was in her seventies and could hardly walk, but did she put on a show. It was hard to believe that she had made her first appearance in the Ziegfeld Follies in 1909, first recorded what became her theme song, "Some of These Days," in 1911, and was still making television appearances on Ed Sullivan and The Tonight Show in the 1950's and early 1960's. What a career and what a charming woman. I used to choke up from emotion every time she spoke. We got along great, and I had the pleasure of escorting her to the stage every night. Rather than coming out from the backstage area, she always made a grand entrance from the front door of the Imperial Room, making her way to the piano with her arm entwined in mine.

She had a wonderful time with us. Sam Shopsowitz sent her matzoh ball soup every day from his Shopsy's deli. Sophie had heard the room was a good place to perform, but she too wanted to make it more intimate. "I want to see no dance floor at all. I want tables, and lots of them, right up to the stage. That way the folks will enjoy me more and I'll enjoy them." She also insisted that all the waiters had to be out of the room while the show was on.

She was right. She vindicated my judgment to management and also taught me a lot of lessons. When a great artist is in the room concentrating all his or her energies on giving the audience pleasure, then the audience must respond in like manner. No talking. No tinkling of spoons. No needless scurrying around by either the staff or the guests. It was an attitude toward the stars that became the hallmark of the Imperial Room.

Sophie packed the place every night and got standing ovations when an ovation still meant something. She was scheduled to come back, but sadly, died of lung cancer before she could.

Whatever lessons I learned from her I had reinforced by the first really big contemporary superstar to appear, Peggy Lee. When she arrived, she told us what to do in no uncertain terms. She even forced us to raise the quality of our sound system and lights. Peggy insisted that all the candles on the tables be extinguished and that there be no service for five minutes before the show and absolutely no

Peggy Lee

service during it. I could understand that. Before, the star would be up there on stage and late-comers would be trying to get served while a waiter might be flaming a Steak Diane.

I brought it to her attention that people might accidentally cut their hands without any light on their table. But she insisted that's the way it had to be. The candles could detract from her stage lighting, which had to be absolutely perfect, especially with the song "Fever," which she performed in a single spotlight and with colors changing with every drum riff.

I soon found out how seriously she took her edict: "There's to be no waiter service while I'm performing." On her opening night, one of our captains, trying to please a guest, leaned around a column to discreetly place a bottle of wine on a table near ringside. In Las Vegas, the waiters crawl under the tables to deliver wine. Peggy saw the hand. She demanded a meeting the next day and said she was going to cancel the show. But we smoothed things out and everything went great the rest of the week. She left me a photograph signed: "To my favorite candle man." That Christmas, I got a card from her saying, *"Louis: Have very merry Christmas. Light all the candles. Love, Peggy."*

The entertainment policy started to make the Imperial Room a major Toronto attraction again. It was such an undeniable success that the hotel management decided to make some very much-needed improvements, not only in the facility but in the menu and service. In 1965, we closed for a month for renovations. The character of the place remained intact, but we added a stage extension that could be rolled out to accommodate artists who needed more space for their act or more musicians than we usually had. We also added a new raised level at the south end, cutting off some of the dance floor while expanding the seating capacity to about 400. The room was given what I thought was a nice new paint job too, although Mr. Buck Crump, Chairman and CEO of Canadian Pacific Limited walked in one day, looked around, and said, "It looks like a laundromat." It was repainted the next day.

In the summer of 1965, Chef Marcel Didier and I also went to New York and Chicago to visit similar establishments to see how they handled things. In a whirlwind tour, we went to smaller restaurants and nightclubs and legendary places like the Copa Cabana, the Persian Room at the Plaza Hotel (which was very similar to the Imperial Room, though it could only seat about twenty-five), the Empire Room at the Waldorf Astoria, Maxim's at the Astor Tower, and the Pump Room at Chicago's

Ambassador Hotel. (I stayed a little longer in Chicago since Nelson Eddy was about to begin an engagement in the Empire Room at the Palmer House. My wife, Corinne, flew in from Toronto so we could take in his openingnight. I sent my card backstage and after the show, Nelson came to our table and spent a wonderful hour with us, telling delightful stories.)

During our tour, Marcel and I talked to captains and Maitre D's, reviewed the service and cuisine, found out what they did to make their artists and audiences happy, and explored any and every aspect of top-of-the-line establishments (and some that turned out to be not that good at all). We had some great meals too.

We were learning. When we reopened, we had a smaller dinner menu and had refined the style of service we offered. We had a new appreciation for the standards we aspired to, especially with the entertainment. My view was that if someone went to their neighbor and said they'd been at the Imperial Room and the neighbor wasn't envious, then the show wasn't worth going to.

After the renovations, we reopened the room with great fanfare, bringing in the fine singer and actress Julie London. She seemed like a good choice to express the more intimate atmosphere we were after. After her first recording, "Cry Me a River," became such a big hit in the mid-fifties, anyone who thought of her at all thought of a warm, dark, smoky, and sultry mood.

Unfortunately, she was a big disappointment. She was so intoxicated on stage almost every night she could barely move around. I kept wondering whether we'd have to cancel a performance and help her off. The one bright spot in her very rough run was that Lorne Greene came in one night with a party of eight. He was riding high on his "Bonanza" fame at the time, but I knew Lorne from when he was at the CBC in the forties and fifties and he'd often come in for lunch. I went over both to say hello and to apologize. I said, "Every night she's just falling all over." Lorne took command of the situation, going up on stage and spending almost an hour with her, helping Julie through the act. I was grateful to Lorne and very upset with Julie, who at least left me a 40-ounce bottle of Crown Royal as a peace offering and parting gift.

She wasn't the only performer with an idiosyncrasy that I and the rest of the staff had to try hard not to notice or say anything about. Frank Fontaine, a well-regarded comedian, knocked back five or six doubles before he'd go on stage. Rodney Dangerfield, who was years away from super-stardom at the time, would disappear into the bathroom with his briefcase for a half hour before every performance. No one ever asked him why. We just gave him "respect."

All through the late sixties and into the seventies, we did get some criticism for the talent we booked. Some newspaper writers thought many of the artists we had were nothing to write home about or, more importantly, nothing to spend a lot of money on. They often weren't the top-notch stars we wanted to get and the ones we eventually had, Peggy Lee being the major exception during these years. We also wanted to present a mix of younger, up-and-coming performers and some of the older artists, some of them legends, who had wide name recognition.

Many of the people we had may have been B-level talent, but they were the stars available at the time, the ones who were well established and played around the circuit of the St. Regis in San Francisco, the Persian Room in New York, the Empire Room at the Palmer House in Chicago, and a place in Detroit or Houston, interrupted by guest spots with Ed Sullivan or on other shows. They were still stars, even if some of them were fading fast.

Many had been in the movies and hit the road when their film careers ended. They were just people who loved to entertain and couldn't or didn't want to do anything else. They used their name and made money, and why not? Audiences still loved them. I stood in line at the Casino Theatre in Toronto to see many of them perform in the 1940's, and I still loved them too. Besides, the Imperial Room was getting right up there with the other great clubs of North America, and in Toronto we were the only game in town. Most of them filled the room. I was privileged not only to see them night after night, but to get to know many of them and become friends. I loved it.

The Showcase

Allan Jones

Of all the people I loved in the movie musicals of the thirties and forties, Allan Jones was second only to Nelson Eddy. Allan had an interesting career, playing romantic leads in the Marx Brothers movies, "A Night at the Opera" and "A Day at the Races." and playing big roles in "Showboat" and especially "The Firefly" with Jeanette MacDonald. That was the movie where he introduced the song he was always associated with, "Donkey Serenade."

He had an outstanding tenor voice and was a wonderful man. Age didn't seem to affect the power of his voice, which was always big. When he first rehearsed on our stage I said, "Mr. Jones, please, with those high notes, the chandeliers are going to fall down and shatter."

He laughed and launched into a beautiful, piercing high note. His wife, Irene Hervey, came with him when he appeared at the Imperial Room, and I was blessed to be able to spend a great deal of time with them. They were lovely people. They visited Toronto a few times later on and always came by to see me.

Jack Jones

Jack Jones, Allan and Irene's son, didn't have the personality his dad had and was not as friendly as Allan either -- at least not at first. But we had him several times and our relationship improved the more I got to know him. His dad had told him all about me.

Jack was a big star, but he seemed troubled. Something was always bothering him, whether a little cold or some other ailment he felt would affect his performance, though he usually went on with the show. One time, however, he came to me in the afternoon and told me he was too sick to go on that night. We were sold out for both shows. Much as I hated to do it, I said we'd cancel them. All my staff and I went through as many telephone numbers as we could for the 800 people we were expecting and told them not to come. After that, he became much warmer to me.

During one of his visits, he brought his girlfriend at the time, actress Susan George, who was very gracious and pleasant. I dined with her every night of the week while he was performing. It was quite a shock and sort of embarrassing when I later saw her with no clothes on in the movie "Straw Dogs."

Jack performed in Toronto in the late nineties and, I heard later when he was on stage he said, "Anyone know what happened to my good friend, Louis Jannetta?" Someone called out, "He's alive." I got a call from him later that night.

Peter Palmer

One of the first singers we had under the new policy was Peter Palmer who was pretty popular at that time. He was a handsome man with a very good voice who had starred in "L'il Abner" on Broadway and in the movies. He was a regular on American TV variety programs. He put on a nice show and posed no problems for me whatsoever.

We became quite friendly, and when I went to New York a few years later, he took me backstage at the theater where he was playing and introduced me to Carol Channing. Then he took me to Sardi's, with its showbiz crowd and its walls covered with photos of all the stars who visited. I thought that was a great idea so I put it in the back of my mind for future reference. When he and his lovely wife, a Canadian from the north, came back to Toronto, we enjoyed another very pleasant evening together.

Mickey Rooney

Mickey Rooney and Don Winslow

Of all the movie stars I enjoyed in my youth, Mickey Rooney held a special place in my memory. When I was eight years old, I cried my eyes out watching "Boys' Town." I loved his musicals with Judy Garland throughout the forties. To my mind, he was a superstar, yet another performer I idolized almost as much as Nelson Eddy.

He came to the Imperial Room early in 1966 with Don Winslow, his partner in a comedy team. They sang, they danced, and they did great comedy routines. I thought the performance was very good. The critics didn't necessarily agree. A couple of them were favorable, but the critic for the Toronto Star, Peter Harris, wrote a scathing review, saying Mickey's act was "embarrassingly awful." I couldn't believe it. The phrase was repeated in the weekend's Star Week guide, which hurt the room and probably hurt the star.

The next time Peter Harris came in, I took him aside, put him up against the wall by my desk, and said, "How could you write such horrible things about someone who gave us so much pleasure over the years? A guy who's still out there working his heart out?" He told me he was not responsible for the headlines at the beginning of the review.

Mickey didn't let it get to him. He was very nice, a kind, wonderful, and gentle man, though he seemed a bit lonely. He stayed at the hotel during his run and would come by in the afternoon to say hello and chat, which was quite a thrill for me. He wanted to bet on the horses and often asked me how to do it, seeing as how gambling was illegal in Ontario at the time. I gambled a lot, but never on the horses. I never knew any bookies, so I couldn't help him out.

Some years later, he came to town to perform in "Sugar Babies" at the O'Keefe Centre and sent me some tickets. The show was very good, and afterwards an usher took me backstage. When Mickey saw me, he hugged me and said, "Louis, you got fat."

I said, "Mickey, so did you."

Van Johnson

Van Johnson was a movie actor I had admired for a long time, though I thought of him more as a dramatic actor than a musical performer. I think I must have put the MGM musicals he did with June Allyson or Esther Williams out of my mind. I remembered him as the typical hero in a bunch of war movies. But he was something of an old-style hoofer, always wearing bright red socks to draw attention to his feet.

His act was okay. He sang and he danced, but didn't do either of them all that well in my view. He was no Fred Astaire or Donald O'Connor. He did good business though. Lots of people obviously remembered him fondly. Our relationship started well, but he turned out to be a difficult character. On the last night of his run, he got mad at me for some reason but never told me why. I always thought that if there was a problem, the artist should be open and honest and direct about it. But Van just fumed and sulked. When the show was over, neither of us said goodbye.

Rudy Vallee

Rudy Vallee was another one of our first big stars, though he hadn't been that big of a star for decades. He was a name but as an entertainer, he was terribly passé. It showed. A regular guest who was a personal friend of Rudy's reserved a table for eight every night of the run so she could bring all her friends. The opening night show was so horrible she cancelled the other reservations. It didn't get any better the rest of the run. I tried to warm up the audience, but he left them cold. Every night I went around to every table where there were people I knew, saying, "You better laugh tonight. Otherwise, when we have a good show, you'll be sitting in the back."

Some years later, Rudy came back to Toronto, performing at the O'Keefe Centre with other legends from the thirties such as Ruby Keeler, Zazu Pitts, and a somewhat younger fellow, Henny Youngman. Afterwards, they all came to a party we had for my old friend, Shopsey. I invited Rudy to come and see the late show of the performer at the Imperial Room that week. He came to an early show with a party of five. They dined, then all stayed for the late show too. At the end of the night, the waiter gave him the check for the meals, but, in deference to his celebrity, I made sure there was no cover charge for either show. The next night he appeared on a local television saying how cheap that Maitre D' Louis Jannetta was, "Inviting us to a show and making us pay our own bill."

Rich Little

Rich Little was just in the early stages of his career when he came to the Imperial Room. He was fairly well known in Canada after starting to make club appearances in Ottawa, where he was born. But it was his appearance on "The Judy Garland Show" in 1963 that made him a name big enough to be worthy of the room. His much more substantial success would come later.

I thought he was a terrific guy as well as an absolute master of mimicry. He really seemed to become the people he impersonated, not only with their voices but with their physical movements and mannerisms. The biggest laughs were for his portrayal of the Canadian prime ministers of the late fifties and early sixties, John Diefenbaker and Lester Pearson. I heard he used their voices for characters in a cartoon show in the States, but the producer thought they were too over-the-top. In our case, some people from the provincial government seemed to think the impersonations were too disrespectful. A couple of them got quite upset and sent a notice to the hotel that he should stop. He didn't, though he did curtail it a bit. The rest of his act was so fantastic it didn't matter much anyway.

We had him three times in the 1960's, although he didn't sell out the place. We were going to book him again but he wanted more money, so he worked the Hook and Ladder Club in the north end of town which featured quite a few artists we didn't want any more. I got a call from someone who saw his act there, telling me that when he came out on stage he said, "There's something missing here. Oh, yeah. Louis." Then he twisted his hand as Maitre D's are supposed to do when palming money. This was a sore point with me, so I called him to object. As far as I know, he never did it again.

Anne Murray

Sometimes Moxie Whitney booked acts I had never heard of. One example in 1970 was a young woman from the Maritimes named Anne Murray. I thought, "Who's this?" I learned soon enough. She had just recorded "Snowbird" and it had become a big, big hit. When her name was advertised, the phone started ringing constantly for reservations.

She shocked me, however, when she came out on stage barefoot and with a backup group that looked like they had just wandered out of the wilderness. I was dumbfounded. Our band musicians and many of the guests were all dressed in tuxedos. The look of her and her crew was new for us. It was a good lesson, though. We began realizing that show business was changing and we had to change with it.

In the late sixties, when Anne Murray performed, only 150 people showed up for the second show, but a lot of people didn't want to leave from the first show. Since we were always afraid of embarrassing the customer in any way, I went to Anne and said, "You'll have to hold up the show for a bit. I've got a problem." I had all my staff bring down 200 chairs from the convention floor upstairs, spread them around the room, then brought everyone in and sat them down and didn't charge them a cover. After that, I made a point of telling people they could only stay for one show or they'd have to pay another cover charge. But I never told people to leave, even if the second show was sold out. That's probably one reason I lasted so long. Everyone got in, even if I did feel like ripping out what was left of my hair to manage it. I always felt the room should be as full as possible, bringing it to their attention that they were welcome to stay for the second show without an additional cover charge.

Anne later appeared at the Royal Alexandra Theatre, the first singer to be booked there. My wife and I were invited to the party after the show. When she saw me, she came over with outstretched arms and said, "Louis, I look different, don't I?"

I said, "Yeah, and you're wearing shoes."

Frank Sinatra

Trini Lopez & Frank Sinatra

Trini Lopez

* These photos are public domain; used for promotional services and not the property of author or publisher.

Trini Lopez was a very talented guy, a Mexican-American who had been signed to a Reprise Records contract by the label's owner, none other than Frank Sinatra. His first album had a song, "If I Had a Hammer," that really took off. He had a good run at chart stardom when he followed that up with "Lemon Tree" and "La Bamba." He'd also done some acting on TV and in the movies, most notably in "The Dirty Dozen" with Lee Marvin and Charles Bronson and a raft of other mid-level stars.

He drew very good crowds to the Imperial Room. He sang well and played guitar and put on a pretty good show, so we had him back several times. We had lunch together often and I was backstage with him a lot, so we got to know each other and had a genial relationship.

One incident during one of his appearances stands out in my memory. 'The Happy Hooker,' Xaviera Hollander, would occasionally come to see the stars. This wasn't the happiest thing for the Imperial Room, especially since some guests at the elevated tables behind the rails told me they could look down and see her hands-under-the-table antics with her dinner companions. But I couldn't keep her

Gordon Cardy, Louis, & Trini Lopez

out and she was generally pretty pleasant. She did have a habit of trying to give her book about life in the sex trade to the performers. One time she got up from her table and I stopped her halfway across the dance floor from giving a copy to Myron Cohen, who probably wouldn't have appreciated it. She did manage to get one to Trini, however, who was a different kind of a guy. I think he probably enjoyed it.

He was a nice fellow, but pretty vain. He loved himself and took himself much too seriously. Miguel Alemin, president of Mexico in the late forties and early fifties, was in the room one night, negotiating a deal with Mr. Donald Curtis, Chairman of Canadian Pacific Hotels at the time, to take over the Acapulco Royale from the Hilton chain. I went backstage and said, "Come out to the front. There are people you should meet. We can show a little respect to a former president of your country." Trini followed me to the president's table.

He said, "I don't go out to the audience for anybody. Frank Sinatra doesn't go out to the audience."

I said, "Trini, you're no Frank Sinatra."

Carmen Cavallaro

* These photos are public domain; used for promotional services and not the property of author or publisher.

Carmen Cavallaro, who first came to the Imperial Room in 1971, was a favorite of mine. Carmen was great, an accomplished classical musician who at one time was known as "The Poet of the Piano." I'd listened to him on the radio and had seen him in the musical revue films like "Hollywood Canteen" that he'd made in the forties. I also enjoyed his work when he played the piano for the soundtrack of "The Eddy Duchin Story" starring Kim Novak and Tyrone Power. Most critics thought he played the music much better than Duchin ever did. He inspired other popular pianists of the era, from Liberace to Roger Williams.

He took his music seriously, practicing eight hours a day every day while he was at the hotel. He took the music so seriously that he didn't want anyone dancing while he played. One embarrassing moment for me came when the premier of Ontario, John Robarts, got up with his wife and started to dance. I had to go over and, in front of a full room, ask them to please sit down as I escorted them back to their table.

Carmen came several times. My major problem with him was that after he finished his act, people would ask for more and he'd do encore after encore. One is great and even two might be okay, but he did far too many of them. He also used the word "goddamn," a first for the Imperial Room. That being a much more innocent time, I was shocked. And it wasn't just me. I thought he lost the audience's respect he'd built up over the previous hour.

Tessie O'Shea

It was rare for the Imperial Room to feature entertainers in the old-style British music hall tradition. But we made an exception for Tessie O'Shea. Audiences knew her mainly from television appearances, though she had a hilarious and memorable role in the movie, "The Russians Are Coming, The Russians Are Coming," and did well on Broadway too, winning a Tony Award in the early sixties.

She was a huge woman with a personality to match. The words "happy" and "hearty" could have been coined just for her and her act. She was a delightful lady and great fun. She sang bawdy songs and did a wonderful rendition of "I've Got a Lovely Bunch of Coconuts." Her good humor and enthusiasm were infectious, and audiences always got into the spirit of the rollicking good times she inspired.

Josephine Baker (with Louis and Ingrid Bergman)

Of the several 20th century legends who came to the Imperial Room—Sophie Tucker, Ginger Rogers, and Marlene Dietrich among them—Josephine Baker had to be one of the most fascinating.

While she started out in American vaudeville, "The Black Venus," as she was known in her heyday, took Europe by storm when she danced almost naked in Paris in 1925.

It was almost 50 years later when she appeared on our stage. She didn't dance erotically in a skirt made of bananas as she did in the twenties, but she almost could have done so. She was 66 years old, but had the body of an 18-year-old. She told me that was due to drinking pickle juice every day.

She hadn't performed much in the sixties and seventies, but financial problems had put her back on the road. She hadn't lost her edge. She put on an energetic and very entertaining show that attracted very good audiences.

One person who came to see her show was Ingrid Bergman, who was in town performing in a Bernard Shaw play at the Royal Alexandra. It was a delightful surprise for me when she came to the door. Knowing she was married to Roberto Rossellini for many years, I spoke to her in Italian and she responded the same way. After the show, I arranged for her to meet with Josephine backstage. Photographers went crazy, capturing for posterity the meeting of two great legends.

Miss Bergman was so pleased, the next day she sent over an invitation for my wife and me to see her own show, with two tickets four or five rows from the front. Corinne couldn't go, so I took my daughter, Patti. What with me being tired and the play being Shaw, Patti had to nudge me every five minutes to stop my snoring. After the curtain calls, her manager escorted us backstage. It was thrilling for me to be there, just the three of us in her dressing room. I loved every movie she ever made. She made us feel so welcome and thanked me again for arranging the meeting with Josephine. She was such a star.

Liberace

Mr. Don Curtis, who was chairman of the Canadian Pacific Hotels, was a good friend of Seymour Heller who was Liberace's manager. One time Liberace was performing at the O'Keefe Centre when he was staying at the Fairmont Royal York Hotel. In the afternoon, Liberace would go to the Walkers House Hotel for a late lunch and I would visit my friend Peter Hackenburg, the hotel manager, so I would go and talk to Liberace when he was finished his lunch. On this day I invited him to come to the Imperial Room when his show was finished. As it happened it was his birthday that week. With the help of Don and Seymour we arranged for a small celebration for Liberace's birthday.

Our pastry chef prepared a beautiful cake in the shape of a piano. Dick Haymes was appearing in the Imperial Room and agreed to sing "Happy Birthday" to Liberace as I presented the beautiful cake.

A picture was taken for the occasion including Don Curtis, Dick Haymes, Liberace and myself.

The next year I went to New York and Liberace was appearing at the Radio City Music Hall Theatre. Mr. Heller not only arranged a great seat for me to see the show, but arranged that I could go backstage and say hello to Liberace.

Liberace expressed his thanks for the little party I had for him. It was a wonderful evening and I enjoyed an extremely talented musician, Liberace, who gave me a wonderful memory that I would not forget.

Dick Haymes

* This photo is public domain; used for promotional services and not the property of author or publisher.

In his time Mr. Haymes was nearly as popular as Frank Sinatra. Dick was married to Rita Hayworth and Joanne Dru. Not at the same time of course. He had made a number of movies, while his specialty seemed to be musicals. One of the most famous, in my opinion, was "State Fair" with Jean Craine. It was very nice of him to sing "Happy Birthday" that evening to Liberace and he was a joy to have at the Imperial Room.

Roy Orbison

I was very excited when Roy Orbison was booked. Needless to say, we were sold out for the whole week. Roy was always very nice and polite to me, so it surprised me when, the last night of his performance, I was called into his dressing room. As it turned out, his manager told me that they had not yet received payment for the week's performances. The policy at the time was to pay for the entertainment booked on the second to last night of performing.

They informed me that they would not be able to perform because payment was not received. It was Friday night; I knew the accounting office was closed. I was thankful that I had built a nice relationship with Roy, his musicians, and his manager. I completely understood their point; however, I explained that the Fairmont Royal York was part of the Canadian Pacific formerly. C.P. built most of the railways and hotels across Canada and as such there was no way that they would not get their money.

Roy and his manager reconsidered and performed that evening. I personally made sure they received payment the next morning.

The Big Bands

Booking the big bands that enjoyed their greatest success between the late 1930's and the early 1950's was usually a gamble. A lot of bands were available. They always found some place to play, even when their leaders had passed on. The Glenn Miller Band stayed on the road for half a century after Miller was lost in the war, and there must have been 20 Dorsey bands around the world under different conductors at various times.

Most bands came to be listened to, not to be danced to. What worked best in the Imperial Room was an act that everyone could enjoy, not just a small group of aficionados who would go to jazz clubs anywhere to hear their favorites. All through the 1970's and into the 1980's, we had some of the biggest name bands in the business, often for two weeks at a time. They usually did pretty well, though they stopped selling out after a couple of engagements.
I got along well with all of them and made some pretty good friendships with some. Their musicians had a reputation as big partiers but, while a few enjoyed life a little more than some others, most were very quiet backstage, real professionals who showed a lot of discipline. They needed discipline to survive constant travel on the road.

Duke Ellington

Duke Ellington, without a doubt, was the best of the bunch. Duke was a genius, not only a great performer, but a composer whose brilliance was recognized around the world. I was never that much of a jazz fan or even a big band fan, but it was impossible not to know and love tunes like "Take the A Train," "Mood Indigo," or "Sophisticated Lady."

His band had some of the best musicians around. Johnnie Hodges was one of the greatest saxophone players and Duke would always single him out to do a couple of numbers. Paul Gonzales was a great sax man too and he'd go around the room on his extended solos, though he overdid the alcohol a bit and many nights had trouble walking.

Duke was a character, always kissing people three times in greeting, once on each cheek and once on the forehead. He loved ice cream and sometimes would look for it at three in the morning. We never had a problem unlocking the kitchen just for him, and many nights I'd stay with him as he devoured bowl after bowl. He was a delightful man and one of a kind. We had him perform three or four times.

I visited him at the Rainbow Room in New York. After the show he came to my table and stayed for a while. We had a good chat.

Cab Calloway

Cab Calloway was of the same vintage as Duke Ellington, and had even succeeded Duke at the Cotton Club in Harlem in the 1930's. He was a character too, with his "zoot suits" and "reet pleats," strutting around singing his trademark song, "Minnie the Moocher," doing his "Heidi-heidi-heidi-ho" routine that was always a good crowd pleaser. He knew how to entertain and had worked on Broadway, starring with Pearl Bailey in the all-black revival of "Hello, Dolly." I remembered him best from his appearance in the great movie, "Stormy Weather."

The hotel's general manager, Gordon Cardy, loved Cab so we brought him in for a regular run as well as for a New Year's engagement. He was a nice fellow, but he couldn't move around much. What you see on television or in the movies is not what you see in front of a live audience. He was quite elderly, but he still put on a good show for an adoring audience.

Count Basie

Many people who know swing-era jazz much better than I do consider Count Basie the most outstanding representative of the big band type -- after the Duke, of course. He really set the music world on fire in the 1930's with his Kansas City style. Even a kid like me in Toronto's Little Italy couldn't help but hear pieces like "One O'clock Jump" and "Jumpin' at the Woodside."

Like a lot of bands, Basie's had a down period in the early fifties, but he came back big time as an elder statesman of jazz and recorded with many great sidemen and singers. I knew him best for his recordings with Frank Sinatra. They were an unbeatable combination.
He was a little frail when he appeared at the Imperial Room, and we'd have to bring him up to the stage in a wheelchair the public never saw. But his fingers still flew across the keyboard. Backstage, he was a gentle man, very quiet and unassuming. It was a pleasure to make his acquaintance. The Count spent quite a few afternoons in the Imperial Room with me.

Artie Shaw

We were very fortunate to book Artie Shaw into the Imperial Room on what was his first tour in decades (and, I think, his last). No one had heard any new music from him in years, but his name alone brought in very good audiences.

He was such a celebrity at the height of his fame in the 1940's. Young people, like me at the time, danced to "Star Dust" and "Frenesi" and "Begin the Beguine." His music was fabulous. Young men especially gave him a lot of respect for the women he had relationships with back in those days—Ava Gardner, Lana Turner, Rita Hayworth, Betty Grable—if not always for his eight marriages, good Catholics that we were. He was the biggest star of the whole Swing Era, yet he just walked away from it all when he was at the very top. It's hard to believe, but he simply grew to hate the music business and hate his fans too.

He brought in a band that was basically made up of young musicians. He just fronted the group. I think everyone was disappointed he didn't play his clarinet, but he had put that away for the last time, publicly at least, in 1954. He wasn't the handsome guy he had been in his prime—he had no hair, for one thing, but then again, neither did I—but he was a very nice man and one of the most popular big band attractions we ever had.

Woody Herman

Woody Herman and his Herds were legendary, and everybody who was around in the 1940's and 1950's knew tunes like "Woodchoppers' Ball" and "Caldonia." Even I could tell that many of his arrangements were influenced by Duke Ellington. He could really swing, and he kept swinging even as music changed so dramatically in the 1960's. Woody always used good, young musicians, leaving his band open to new ideas.

His music was more jazz than big band, and the Imperial was never noted for jazz but he did some business, especially the first time he appeared. He was a very pleasant man to deal with and never let his burdens get the best of him. He had so many tax problems he had to keep working even when I suspect he wouldn't have minded taking life a little easier.

Buddy Rich

Buddy Rich made his first appearance at the Imperial Room in 1970 and came back in 1983 with Joe Williams. That second engagement was the most memorable, especially for jazz fans. Joe Williams was one of the greatest jazz singers of all time and Buddy was the greatest drummer. Even Gene Krupa said Buddy was "the greatest drummer ever to have drawn breath." He'd played with some of the best band leaders in the world before he formed his own groups.

Buddy was a real tough guy, a black belt who just hammered on his musicians, most of whom were pretty young. He petrified them in rehearsals, was very demanding, and had a scathing sense of humor. I found him more congenial. We developed a pretty good relationship, especially after I arranged to get him six of the best seats at a Blue Jays baseball game against his beloved Baltimore Orioles. I went with him to the game, and he didn't even mind that we cheered for different sides.

Guy Lombardo and his brother, Ebert

Few people defined or symbolized the hotel dining room tradition of the first half of the 20th century as much or as well as Guy Lombardo. His fame and influence started to be felt long before my time, of course. He and his brothers, Carmen and Lebert, and other musicians in The Royal Canadians left their hometown of London, Ontario, in 1924. Guy and his band took up residence in the Roosevelt Hotel in New York City in 1929 and stayed for thirty years.

All the time I was growing up, everyone listened to him at the Roosevelt on radio every New Year's Eve. He was an institution, a big part of New Year's celebrations across North America. He started the tradition of playing "Auld Lang Syne," still a standard element of New Year's celebrations to this day.

After I took charge of the Imperial Room, I often thought of booking Guy and his band, though not on New Year's. We had our own traditions at the Royal York and, besides, Guy continued his usual broadcasts from the Waldorf Astoria right up until 1976 (having left the Roosevelt after 1959). The management and I talked about it quite a lot in the 1960's. We thought it would be nice to have him, but we doubted whether we could afford him, so nothing was ever done.

In 1969, he was playing an engagement in Toronto and happened to be staying at the Royal York. I heard he was having a meal in the Black Knight restaurant, so I decided to take the bull by the horns. I went down, introduced myself, and said, "Would you mind coming up to the Imperial Room? It would be an honor to show you the room."

He was very gracious and came with me immediately. As he looked over the room with a professional eye, I explained that since we'd moved to the star format, we had booked some bands and were booking more. Our problem was that these bands (Duke Ellington and Woody Herman were both scheduled to perform in 1970) were groups people liked to listen to rather than dance to. We could have lots of tables to cover the costs. I said, "I know with you, Mr. Lombardo, people would come to dance. We'd have to create a bigger dance floor. And you are kind of expensive, sir. I don't know whether we could get enough people in."

He waved off my concern. "Louis, the tighter they are, the better they like it."

We booked him for November, 1970. While we did enlarge the dance floor to some extent, sure enough, he was right. When he played, everyone danced everywhere -- on the broadloom, between tables, on every free spot all over the room. After that, he opened the room for us in mid-September every year but one from 1971 to 1976. His shows almost always sold out right up until the end.

His fan base in Toronto and southern Ontario generally was huge. We especially used to get many people from London, Ontario. They'd send requests up to the bandstand, send him personal notes, and talk to him every chance they got. Quite a few said they went to school with him or reminded him of when they met him in some dance hall in the old days. He was always cordial and courteous, saying, "Oh, sure. Yes, how are you?"

I was very impressed with his memory. As a Maitre D', of course, a good memory was one of my most important and powerful traits, so I asked him about it. "Guy, I'm amazed. How do you remember all these people?"

He said, "I don't remember anything from fifty years ago. I don't know who they are."

He was a fine gentleman and about the most respected person in the industry. He was a tough man too. I found that out when, during one of his appearances, he heard that his drummer had been quoted in the press making gentle fun of the Lombardo sound and criticizing the band's style, saying Guy's music was too old for him. The drummer, who was a very good musician, was also Guy's nephew. That didn't matter. Guy fired him the same day. I was shocked and said, "That must have been hard for you."

He said, "No. I've worked too hard for too many years to do what I've done and get where I am. Nobody talks that way."

We developed a good personal relationship over the years, becoming friends. Every year he'd send me a "Happy New Year" telegram and we'd get together whenever he was in town. He liked the fights, and if there was a good bout scheduled at Maple Leaf Gardens—one between Jose Napolos and Clyde Gray comes to mind—I'd call the promoter to make sure Guy and I had ringside seats.

He was living on Long Island in those years and I had the privilege of being an overnight guest at his home. He was a great boater and an important figure in hydroplane racing, winning several big races in the 1940's. He proudly showed me his hardware and mementoes. He also produced musicals every year at Jones Beach, with the cast performing on barges anchored together in the ocean. He took me to see "Fiddler on the Roof."

I have so many good memories from Guy. One of the fondest came about one winter when we were shut down for ten days. Rather than go south for a holiday as Corinne and I usually did, we took a holiday at Toronto's Westbury Hotel. We were celebrating our anniversary and I arranged a party for about twenty of our friends. Guy was staying at the Westbury too, and he came down to spend the entire evening with us, charming the guests as only he could do. He was a real gentleman.

In early November, 1977 I got a phone call from a reporter asking for my reaction to Guy's death. It was the first I had heard of it. I was so shocked, I couldn't speak. Something very special had gone out of my life and out of the world. A number of years later, I appeared in a documentary about his life.

The Responsibilities of a Maitre D' at the Hotel

All the time we were learning how to operate the Imperial Room better as a night club, I was learning how to become a better Maitre D'. I knew all the basics, of course. The experience handling the Black Knight Room as Maitre D' was invaluable. And I'd been in the business a very long time.

I'd watched my friends and mentors, Henry Capri and David Chiasco, in action for years. But there's a lot more to it than the basics.

Some people are a little confused about what a Maitre D' does, probably because of the stereotype seen so often in movies, especially in the 1930's, and on television. At one level, the role of the Maitre D' is pretty clear in the best and most elaborate establishments. The Maitre D' is the guy who's responsible for the overall management of service. A big part of that is the front-of-house position, looking after all operations, whether it's greeting people at the door, catering to the wishes of long-time guests, giving everybody the best table available, and generally making sure everything runs smoothly. In some places, the term "head waiter" means the same thing.

But the stereotyped image of a Maitre D' is of some snooty guy who fawns over the famous and well-to-do and consigns the lesser folks to a table behind a pillar or over by the door to the kitchen where busboys and waiters rattle by all through the night. I've heard many words applied to Maitre D's over the years. "Imperious" came up a lot. "Haughty" and "overbearing" did too.

Admittedly, there's some truth to this image. The position of Maitre D'hotel goes back a long way, to before the French Revolution when the people filling it really were "masters of the hotel" -- the whole hotel, not just a restaurant. Those sorts of people were dealing with aristocrats and royalty. They had to be diplomats and act aristocratically themselves. They were renaissance men. In the European tradition, some still are.

In North America, the image was fixed by the man generally recognized as the first Maitre D' on the continent -- Oscar Tschirky, who became so famous as the Maitre D' at the Waldorf-Astoria Hotel in New York City that he was very widely known for decades as simply "Oscar of the Waldorf." He was the one who introduced the European custom of greeting patrons by name and always taking care of their personal wants, especially for what were known in his day as "the swells." He was a colorful man-about-town and a confidant of financiers and industrialists and stars. He inspired most of the portrayals of Maitre D's in movies during the glamour days when actors were always going into nightclubs, like the Coconut Grove or 21, and bantering with a Maitre D' in a tux who always seemed to have a French, or at least a continental accent. I loved those movies.

Many Maitre D's in Toronto during the sixties and seventies were trained in Europe, some in Switzerland, just like Oscar of the Waldorf. Over there, the training was strict and the Maitre D' was close to a monarch. He moved around with great bearing, surveying everything and everybody, and was always very knowledgeable about foods and wines. He'd line up the kitchen and wait staff before opening every day and inspect their fingernails and uniforms and handkerchiefs to make sure they were clean.

As for me, a lot of people thought I looked more like a bouncer than a Maitre D'. One newspaper article went so far as to say, "There is nothing elegant in the way you'd expect a Maitre D' to be elegant: he has a squat, imposing wrestler's body. He appears uncomfortable in formal clothes." That was a little harsh in my view. I like to think I had a more refined presence. I tried to be elegant all the time. Some of the kinder people said they thought I looked like Mario Lanza. Some of the less kind mentioned Ernest Borgnine.

I was also out of the ordinary in that I was never that astute when it came to food and beverage. I didn't have the knowledge of Swiss Maitre D's with their formal training or many other fine Maitre D's such as John Arena, who ran Toronto's famed Winston's restaurant. My training was the Imperial Room at the Royal York.

As far as the staff was concerned, while I enjoyed making a grand entrance when I first took over the room, I soon put an end to the daily inspection. I thought it was demeaning to grown men and women, many in their thirties or forties or even their fifties, to have to go through that. I just told them to groom themselves as if they were going to a wedding and to welcome guests as if they were welcoming them into their own homes. So I expected them to fuss over every last-minute detail, check all the table settings, arrange the flowers properly, buff up the silver, and whatever else they would do in their homes to make a good impression.

I told the staff their job was to keep the Imperial Room the finest place in North America and to be honest with the guests. We were all there to impress our guests and make their visit a grand experience. The guests didn't have to impress me or anyone else. I think the staff appreciated my approach. They knew I'd organize and plan, but that we were all part of a team. They accepted me as their leader. A Maitre D' has to be a leader.

Any changes I made over the years were to improve the lot of the patrons and, of course, the entertainers. For them, reducing the size of the dance floor was just a start. I did whatever I could to protect them. It was a balancing act. Guests wanted to meet the stars or have them fulfill special requests, so I'd bring those concerns to their attention, knowing the stars would turn the guests down. But I wasn't pushy about it and the stars respected my position. With many stars, I'd throw parties after the performance on behalf of the hotel. Some never forgot.

For the patrons, I wanted to follow through on a Maitre D's major duty: setting the standard of customer service in many ways, big and small. Sometimes it was as simple and straightforward as consulting with the host of a dinner party beforehand and having everything prepared by the time the guests arrived. I was amazed that was considered a big innovation in the 1960's. It seemed like simple common sense to me.

I worked very hard to make sure service on the floor kept to the highest standards. Outstanding service can really set a restaurant apart, especially when there's a lot of competition as there was in Toronto in the 1960's and 1970's. I also worked hard to make sure the pace of service was just right, not too slow and not too fast. When service is choreographed properly, a guest never has to raise a hand for anything. Nobody should have to ask for anything. Some article called me the "Toscanini of the Room" for the way I watched the guests and staff and orchestrated all the "goings-on." From my desk by the door, I could see every one of the 150 tables and could sense if something was wrong. I was fortunate that I knew 80 percent of the people coming to the Imperial Room. It was a steady clientele.

As for the stereotype, I couldn't go around like people saw in the movies with my nose in the air. That would have been ridiculous for a guy who came from Italy at seven with no shoes, sold bananas from a wagon, raked coal, and waited for food on Christmas morning. I wasn't cut out to act high and mighty. I was more suited to taking a personal touch with anybody and everybody.

It's not that I didn't appreciate who I was dealing with most of the time. I had served and greeted the members of the Toronto establishment for three generations. I'd met many of the people who built this great country. I'd met people who brought their kids to dinner and I'd seen those kids grow up and bring their own children to the room so they could learn how to dine out in style.

I was always willing to go the extra mile for regular guests. I knew who was who and how they should be treated. The main thing was to be efficient, complimentary, and always discreet. For the most part, the big business wheeler-dealers, politicians, and celebrities were less demanding than some other customers. They knew what they liked. I got to know what they liked and made sure we gave it to them. If any new special needs came up, I catered to them too. Learning the special tastes and needs of a customer and remembering them as soon as that person walked back in the door was fundamental to perfect service.

It also comes in handy to know other things about the regulars. I used to read the business and financial pages regularly to keep up with what was happening with Bay Street pecking orders, achievements, failures, and sometimes scandals. I never went out of my way to discover the latest gossip, but an awful lot of gossip found its way to me. That was helpful. I didn't want to sit rivals or enemies next to each other.

Every once in a while I'd also be able to phone a regular and discreetly suggest that he and his wife arrange to dine on a different night than the one originally planned. It wasn't unusual for complex romantic relationships to create a tense and frosty atmosphere. That was to be avoided at all costs.

The newer or infrequent customers were more of a challenge. A good Maitre D' always wants to make every guest feel special and make new customers especially feel like old friends. You have to be quick to do that. You have to start noticing things as soon as the guests come in, studying their attitudes, the way they carry themselves, how they approach you, and how they talk and dress. Though the way people dressed became less and less of a good indicator of wants and personality as socializing became more casual and informal. The art of the Maitre D' is the knack of sizing up people accurately and using your judgment quickly, wisely, and well.

That's not easy. Not everybody can be a Maitre D'. To deal with people is not easy. Maitre D's, along with the waiters and captains, have to deal with many kinds of individuals. Some are gracious. Some are noisy, demanding, or difficult. Some are just jerks. Maitre D's have to be clever enough to handle every customer request, even if they're outrageous, and manage every tough situation or unusual incident. Keeping your head in the midst of disorder is a big thing for Maitre D's.

Public relations is the most important part of the job. That means being at the door to greet people when they arrive, calling them by their last names, visiting their table (once) to make sure the service was prompt and efficient and that they enjoyed the food, then being the last person to speak to them on their way out. That leaves a good impression and, besides, you can learn quite a bit about how the restaurant's working that way. It's also a good reason to repeat their names.

Remembering everybody's name takes a lot of practice. There are a few tricks to developing the knack as well, though sometimes the tricks can themselves turn tricky. I was once very embarrassed when a familiar big business executive came to the door and I said, "Good evening, Mr. Razor. It's a pleasure to welcome you back to the Imperial Room."

He said, "Nice to see you again too, Louis. But the name is Shaver."

Personal service was the name of the game, and I did well enough at it that my personality came to be associated with the place, not an unusual thing for a Maitre D' in a venue like the Imperial Room. I set the tone. I can't count how many times some newspaper article or radio or TV commentator effectively said, "Louis is the Imperial Room." One article said that to our regular patrons, I was "as much of a star as the entertainers who perform there."

I worshiped the real stars who came there, so the Imperial Rom became known as very loving of its stars, on and off the stage. I had the pleasure of meeting and getting to know so many great artists and entertainers.

The British actors who came to town to perform at the Royal Alexandra or the O'Keefe Centre became great favorites. I got to know Hayley Mills quite well. She was performing at the Royal Alex when she was still quite young, and she and her husband came to the Imperial Room. I also got to know her father, Sir John Mills. Sir Laurence Olivier would come after performing at the O'Keefe in King Richard. I'd bring him in and sit him at my table where he wouldn't be disturbed. We'd chat a bit then I'd leave him alone to enjoy his meal.

He sent me a nice portrait of himself when he returned to the UK. Sir Ralph Richardson, a very nice man, would come in after a performance at the Royal Alexandra and say, "Good evening, Louis (which he always pronounced 'Lewis,'). How are you?"

"Very well, Your Lordship. Let me make you comfortable."

"No, I'll just stand here beside you." Which is what he usually did -- stand beside me near the door as he listened to the acts.

Sir Ralph Richardson

Many American stars, of both the cinema screen and television, dined in the room. I was often called upon to render some special service, and most were very thoughtful in remembering that service with a gift. Arthur Godfrey, a very powerful man in the early days of television, a star-maker, came to Toronto for many years to open the Royal Winter Fair, riding his palomino horse around with the Toronto horsey set. When he came, he'd dine in the Imperial Room (always with a bottle of Chateau Lafite Rothschild) and see the show. We had many conversations and I got to know him pretty well. One year, he came to my door in a flap because he didn't have buttons for his white vest. I took him up to my office and found three buttons, one larger than the others. A month later, I got a lovely letter with a gift box of mother-of-pearl buttons.

The regular patrons also trusted me to look after them well. Everyone wanted to be at the Imperial Room for a special performer. We were sold out most of the time, but people would call the hostess and say, "Can I talk to Louis?" I'd find a way to get them in. That made me very popular. Other Maitre D's would call too, to see if I could do something for a very important client of theirs. Even if I didn't know them, I would find a way to get their clients in. I felt those of us in the fraternity should look after our own.

This often involved tickets for special events around town. Harold Ballard, who ran Maple Leaf Gardens and the Toronto Maple Leafs hockey club, was very good to me. He'd always ask what I wanted, giving me my choice of tickets. If it was twenty-five-dollar tickets to a Frank Sinatra concert or front row seats to a sporting event, they were mine. I could sell or give away the tickets to friends or regulars. He let me have a hundred tickets to see the Beatles in 1964. I took my kids and sat right up front. I distributed others to the friends I'd grown up with who took all their kids. I knew so many people and made so many people happy.

I regret that wasn't always possible. As people would come in, I'd look at them and sense whether I could make them happy by giving them this or that table. Not everybody could sit ringside. I had physical pain when I had to seat people at bad tables, especially those who regularly supported the room. While the room was making money, we all had a job. There were a few times I got upset at the door, trying to make everybody happy. Some people would offer a fifty- or hundred-dollar bill. I never looked for it, but I wasn't averse to accepting it. They'd ask, "Why can't I have that table?" How could I manage that without antagonizing the guests? A lot of times I thought I had ulcers.

The job was wearying sometimes. Being sensitive to people's needs takes a lot of energy, and the hours were very long, starting before lunch and going until the paperwork wrapped up at two or three in the morning. And that was usually for six days a week. Being on your feet for most of that time—and often on the move—can really test your stamina.

It was sometimes painful too. I remember one year coming down with the flu just before New Year's Eve, our biggest day. I felt like razors were going through my throat whenever I talked, but I lay in bed at home taking reservations and advising the staff. One Christmas, I was leading the procession of the boar's head, the frozen log, and the cherries flambé. The room was completely dark, and as I paraded around the room, I tripped over the steps in front of the stage and rolled over. I was black and blue all over, but I was there every day after, dragging my leg around as I took people to their tables.

Working hard to make a living, working crazy hours, always being nice to people, always giving, always being there—it takes dedication to be the best Maitre D' possible. It's gratifying that even today, after so many years, people haven't forgotten. In that way at least, I was like the other stars our patrons came to see. I was on stage every night of the week, greeting eight hundred people. Everybody watched me as I went around the room. They remember.

I was born to be a Maitre D'. It was fate. That I lasted so long was up to me. Maitre D's often don't last because they get into trouble somehow, overbooking or not riding out changes in management or fashions. Most last three or four years, even in Las Vegas. I'm proud that I went through four Canadian Pacific chairmen—Coleman, then Buck Crump (who really made Canadian Pacific), Senator Sinclair, and Bill Stinson—as well as several chairmen of hotels, a position that came into being later in my career. I went through seven Royal York general managers—Jack Johnson, Angus McKinnon, Gordon Cardy, Chuck Burton, Hans Grubmayr, Timothy Whitehead, and Pierre Bougain—and maybe 20 food and beverage directors.

I missed a lot of things, but that's the price you pay. For forty-eight years, I was never home for Christmas or New Year's Eve or Easter or Mother's Day. Fortunately, two of my daughters, Connie and Patti, were married at the Royal York and given the Royal Suite for their wedding nights. I rarely made it to other family weddings. My brother was very upset about my not getting to the reception for his daughter's wedding on time. I made the ceremony in the morning, but Robert Goulet was opening that night and we had a full house. I could leave it to the staff to look after the second show, but for the opening I felt I had an obligation to the room. Fulfilling it by making sure everyone was at the best table was part of my job. (When I finally walked into the wedding banquet hall, everyone gave me a sarcastic standing ovation.)

I've often been asked if it was worth it. How can I say otherwise, having had the opportunity to meet some of the most powerful, influential, and controversial men and women of the 20th century? Hobnobbing with the talented, rich, and famous was just one aspect of it, though an important part.

Often, when business was slow during the winter months or when an entertainer wasn't as popular as we'd hoped, some of the staff would get disgruntled about not making much money. I'd have a meeting to remind them of all the people in construction working outside in cold weather and how fortunate we all were to be in the wonderful atmosphere of the Imperial Room every night, dealing with business people and doctors and lawyers and professors. Many, just like me, had little education, yet we were able to buy homes and send our children to college. I'd tell them that working the room was an education in itself if they only had the smarts to take advantage of it. In fact, a lot of waiters who left the Imperial Room went far in life because they had learned how to communicate and how to deal with the kind of wonderful guests we had at the room. Many became very successful, owning restaurants, grocery stores, and other businesses. Some even became Maitre D's.

Although the hours were long and a sacrifice for my family, there were also satisfying perks. People did so many wonderful things for me because of my position. I remember standing on the back line at Lichee Gardens, a popular Chinese restaurant. The Maitre D' noticed us near the back and asked my wife and me to follow him to the dining room ahead of the line. People were so generous to me and so kind. I was always given special consideration in theaters and treated with the utmost respect. I'd go to a restaurant and someone would send a bottle of wine to my table.
For someone who never went to high school, let alone college, life was rich, full, and exciting. Becoming known around Toronto as King of the Maitre D's capped everything, especially since it was other Maitre D's, my peers, who gave me the title. It wasn't a title I sought, but I accepted it.

My Introduction into the Stock Market

It was 1942 and I was a fourteen-year-old busboy. David Winchell, who was twelve years old, was taken to the Imperial Room by his father. I was usually busing in this section where they sat. It was easy for the two boys to start a friendship. -- a friendship that has lasted to this day, sixty-six years later.

I was about seventeen and been promoted to a waiter when Mr. Winchell would always ask to be seated in my section so I could wait on him. At fifteen he liked his food, but his favorite dinner was Lobster Newberg, Long-Branch potatoes and heart of lettuce with Roquefort cheese dressing. He knew that I would make it for him whenever he came to the Imperial Room.

Even in the later days when I opened my own restaurant, "Louis Jannetta's Place," he would still eat the same meal. My chefs, Carmelo Mantione and Adam Rogala, knew that when I asked them to prepare that meal, David had arrived.

When I had organized the Canadian Italian Hockey League he immediately gave a five-hundred-dollar donation to the team. In 1947, five hundred dollars was a lot of money.

By 1962, David had become a very successful stock broker and president of a number of companies and I had been crowned as the King of Maitre D's of the Black Knight Room. One day I showed David the four thousand shares on call of a stock that I had. I did not even know what 'on call' meant. David explained that it meant that I was not responsible if the stock went down in price but if it went up, I could sell the stock and receive the profits above what I had originally paid out.

A few months later I went to a stag and there were card games and a crap table as well. I started to shoot dice and I lost quite a bit of money so I went to David and told him I needed some money. I had never confessed my gambling problem to him, so he did not know I had lost all my money to craps.

David said he would arrange to sell my stock, which of course he did and called me to pick up my payment. David broke the stock down and over a few times was able to sell them for me.

One day David called me to meet him at the Toronto airport. He was on his way to New York and wanted to see me before he left. He handed me an envelope filled with cash. I did not open it until I was back home and, to my surprise, inside was fifty-one hundred dollar bills. Dave had told me that he had put some stocks away for me and wanted to surprise me.

That envelope was the last time I ever received any gifts from Dave. He was very upset because he had found out about my gambling habit and instead of using the money he had given me to help my situation, I was losing it at the tables.

I am happy he did so. He was a true friend who refused to help with my gambling problem and to this day we are still the best of friends. It is because of our friendship that I was introduced to every top stock broker, promoter and tycoon in Canada.

I had many great opportunities and made, and sadly lost, a lot of money by listening to many presidents and CEO's in the industry that would tell me things that were 'going' to happen in their companies and dropped tips to obtain stock.

We had grown up together as kids and had made our mark in the world. At the time I did not always take advantage of the tips cast my way and I would have just gambled away my luck. However, in the years to come I bought a lot of stock and sometimes it paid off.

In 1987 I went to Vegas. I was up money and I had planned to leave the next morning as was my habit. But this time I didn't. I stayed and as fast as I had won the night before, I lost my winnings and more. Much more.

I knew when I went home that I was in serious trouble. I would try to make up my Vegas disaster with my stocks. We all know that in 1987 the stock market crashed. Between Vegas and the crash I lost much more than money. Because of that day, I have not gambled since.

All my life I worked very hard and foolishly I gambled all but the money needed to take care of my family. There was always food to eat.

Shirley McClaine

Tammy Wynette

Laine Kazan

Al Waxman

Burton Cummings

Gregory Hines

Jack Benny

Eartha Kitt

Lord Ken Thomson, Ted Lindsay, Louis & Mrs. Lindsay

Sir Lawrence Olivier

Lee Majors

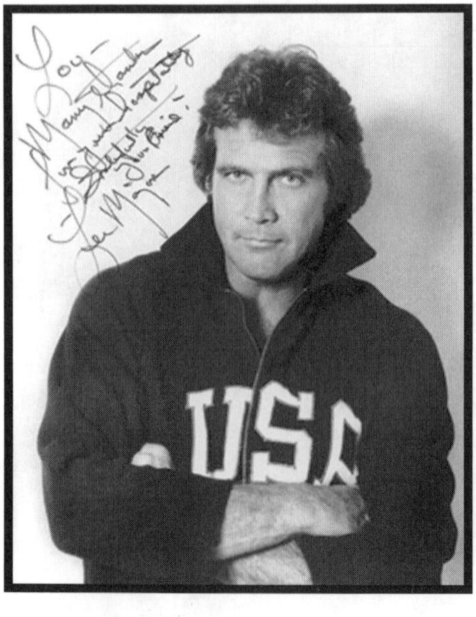

Mimi VanDoren

Ray Charles

Tom Jones

Suzanne Somers

Shirley Jones

Frank Bogart, Louis & Lord Ken Thomson

Sandy Duncan

Michael J. Fox

Roger Miller

Eddy Shack, Louis, Dickie Duff, & Sen. Frank Mahavolich

Sen. Frank Mahavolich, Mayor Miller & Louis

Pains, joys and stars at the Imperial Room

BY LAWRENCE O'TOOLE

Star-gazer Jannetta of the Imperial Room: he now rubs shoulders with the great.

LOUIS JANNETTA, maitre d' of the Imperial Room at the Royal York Hotel, started his career as a busboy in the old Venetian Room of the same hotel. He was 14 then. Now he is beaming as he says that he will celebrate 33 years working there in June.

"When I started working here in the Imperial Room there was no entertainment and I felt the place needed a little more than just supper and dancing. Times were changing so I made some suggestions to Angus McKinnon, the manager, and we tried out Jane Morgan. Things started out slowly but soon the Imperial Room and entertainment became synonymous."

He cringes a little when he remembers the disaster with Rudy Vallee, whose vocabulary was somewhat tarnished and just a little too blue to be accommodated in the red plush of the Imperial Room. "It wasn't only the language, it had a lot to do with Vallee as a performer. He could hardly sing and he couldn't tell jokes. He spent most of his time doing just that and it took us a long time to live that one down." Jackie Vernon was another flop and Yvonne de Carlo almost succeeded in emptying the room one New Year's Eve.

When he talks about Marlene Dietrich his eyes light up and a big smile flashes across his face. He calls her "one of the greatest artists I have ever known." When she performed at the Royal York last year she had broken her leg but he remembers her as a real trouper.

"She was under great stress but she was very professional about it all. She got such a tremendous reception that she promised to come back. At first I was a little wary of her and kept my distance, but once I started talking to her she opened up. I talked about Carole Lombard and Russ Columbo with whom she had appeared in a company and she began reminiscing. She even kissed me once," he says and stops talking for a while. He's beaming again and one supposes he is thinking about the enigmatic Dietrich.

Jannetta comes from the generation that spent its afternoons star-gazing in darkened theatres. "When I was 11 I saw three movies a day. It was one of the greatest thrills of my life when I met Sir C. Aubrey Smith. I'll never forget Lily Pons either. I was only 15 when I met her but I got to know her really well."

He continues talking in an affectionate tone and mentions his friendship with Tony Bennett, whom he can't compliment enough. But there are those who are very difficult to please and the artistic temperament has been a raging stress for the maitre d'. "Artists are so difficult to please, so touchy. They are concerned about everything from lighting to musicians to noise in the room."

Jannetta has been hard put to please everybody. Rubbing shoulders with the great may have its charms but it can be a pain in the neck at times. "Take Frank Gorshin as an example. He's a wonderful guy but he's so unpredictable. He walked off the stage here three times. One night he saw a waiter go to a table during his act and he left."

Jannetta has had to be a confidant and a sometime father figure to most performers. Besides having to remonstrate with Gorshin he says there have been many times when stars come to him with their personal problems. "Vic Damone was unhappy about his girl friend Becky and I had to stay up with him all hours consoling him. Then there was that time when his wife committed suicide."

Most performers have become close friends of the maitre d'. All one has to do is mention Jannetta's name in most supper clubs and one is assured of a good seat and impeccable service. Most of the patrons that come to the Imperial Room have been doing so for years and he claims it's like one big family in the imposing dining room.

It's little wonder that he is so well liked. Jannetta is a beefy man in his late forties with kind eyes and a gregarious disposition. He tries awfully hard to be kind to everyone he talks about. He is also modest to a fault.

This may account for his reluctance to talk about his recent investiture in the Knights of Malta, an Italian award given to those who do charitable work. He has been awarded this honor for his 26 years of work with the Italian Hockey League in Canada. The investiture, which took place last Sunday, was the first ever to be made outside Italy.

He has a way with performers: Sonny and Cher were doing too much ad-libbing in their show but he persuaded them to cut down the talk in their act. He has a nose that senses things out of joint, and he has the kind of diplomacy that rectifies certain problems.

"When Tammy Grimes appeared here she wore a striking silver dress that made her look sensational. The next time she wore a gaudy pantsuit that did little for her figure, and the audience wasn't reacting until her fifth or sixth song. I knew it was the suit so I went backstage and tried to drop a few hints. That didn't work.

"Later I kept saying 'Tammy, what a beautiful dress you wore last year'. That didn't work either. One night she said to me, 'Louis, I hear you didn't like my outfit' and, naturally, I was embarrassed. But she changed into a dress and got better response."

It seems embarrassment is also part of the maitre d' life style. Jannetta was embarrassed when he couldn't keep up with Edward G. Robinson who was talking a mile a minute in Italian. "It was embarrassing because I was born in Italy!" Then there are the instances when a patron must be evicted for unsuitable behavior.

He recalls one instance where one seemingly civilized gentleman kept talking all through Shelley Berman's act. Jannetta tried to reason with him but couldn't. Berman took a more direct course of action—after his act he came down to the table and christened the upstart with a glass of water.

Then there was the time when a woman kept her back to the stage during Kay Ballard's performance. Ballard, not to be outdone, followed the mysterious lady out of the room and told her, in no uncertain terms, what she thought of her. Another time Sonny and Cher's show was held up because another lady made an insulting remark about Cher.

One particular guest who had been disrupting shows and hooting had to be banned from the Imperial Room for two years. Jannetta gave him another chance but the man responded by booing Paul Anka. Jannetta throws up his hands and then adds that the man hasn't been allowed back since.

Jannetta is a kind of performer himself. "Every Italian is a frustrated singer," he says. "I had lessons when I was small and I cried when Mario Lanza died." One night Nelson Eddy insisted that he sing and he did. Since then he has been known to perform for the likes of Lauren Bacall and the cast of Applause. Impressionists mimic him but it seems one night Jack Carter came closest to catching the cadence of his voice and the brio of his actions.

When you talk with him you unearth a treasure trove of information. For example, few people know that the legendary Josephine Baker has a double pickle juice every night or that the late Duke Ellington drank Coca-Cola with two teaspoons of sugar in it.

He admits that performers are in "a world of their own. A lot of them forget everything when they are up on that stage." One feels there is more Jannetta could tell but he doesn't. "You remember the good and you want to forget the bad. Right?"

Corinne Jannetta, Susie Jannetta, Patti Jannetta-Baker & Connie Jannetta-Celebre

Pino & Connie Celebre, Jeanie Flaman, Joseph Celebre, Fern Flaman & Julianna Celebre

Louis & Corinne Jannetta

Louis & puppet in Rome

Frank & Teresa Jannetta, Nadine, Michael, Paul & Frankie Jr.

Louis & his first great-grandson Owen Pickett

NIGHTLIFE

Daddy sees daughter hit the big time

BY BLAIK KIRBY

A proud Poppa's dream came true over the weekend in the plush Imperial Room of the Royal York Hotel. Maitre d' hotel Louis Jannetta saw his daughter Patti perform on the famous stage of "his" room, and do well enough that neither of them need blush over the nepotism that put her there.

Patti is the lead singer and sets the tone for Mixed Reaction, a soft rock and disco quintet that plays places such as Diamond Jim's in Hamilton, or the Camelot on Mount Pleasant Road. It is certainly not famous, and in normal times wouldn't dream of playing the Imperial Room, which belongs to the likes of Tony Bennett and Marlene Dietrich.

Last week, however, the room's scheduled entertainer cancelled out, and Jannetta knew that Mixed Reaction was available. He persuaded the hotel to give Patti and Co. a chance; after all, any entertainment would attract some customers, but none at all would leave the room almost empty. So Mixed Reaction got a booking lasting until tomorrow night.

—Globe and Mail, Barrie Davis

Maitre d'Janetta with Patti; the group moves up to the room where Tony Bennett plays.

The band does not dazzle—but then, nobody expected it to. It does an honest, competent show—carefully omitting its normal disco dance tunes—and Patti not only leads with a strong, stylish voice, but creates a pleasant impression. She looks as if she's enjoying herself, and shows a youthful and likeable personality.

Patti's singing is, to her credit, tasteful and without excesses. She is not yet a knockout interpreter, but gets across a song's meaning well enough, which is the first step. Guitarist, Roy Buna, also gets one solo, putting a gentle touch and some expressiveness into feelings.

The band's main fault is to be blamed largely on its music, and partly on its arrangements. Most pop songs are very dull listening, with the same few words repeated dozens of times—and that's boring. Mixed Reaction could help to relieve this tedium if it found ways of making the arrangements more interesting as the songs plod on.

There is a warm family feeling about musicians, at least when it comes to encouraging youngsters. So several of Howard Cable's house band, made up largely of top studio men, are sitting in the shadows behind Mixed Reaction and tossing in little riffs to help out. Good for them.

Jannetta has a booming voice that can always be heard leading the applause with shouts of "bravo," no matter who the entertainer. This time, who can blame him?

Family Dinner at Louis Jannetta's Place

Louis & Corinne Jannetta, Ashley & Kevin Pickett

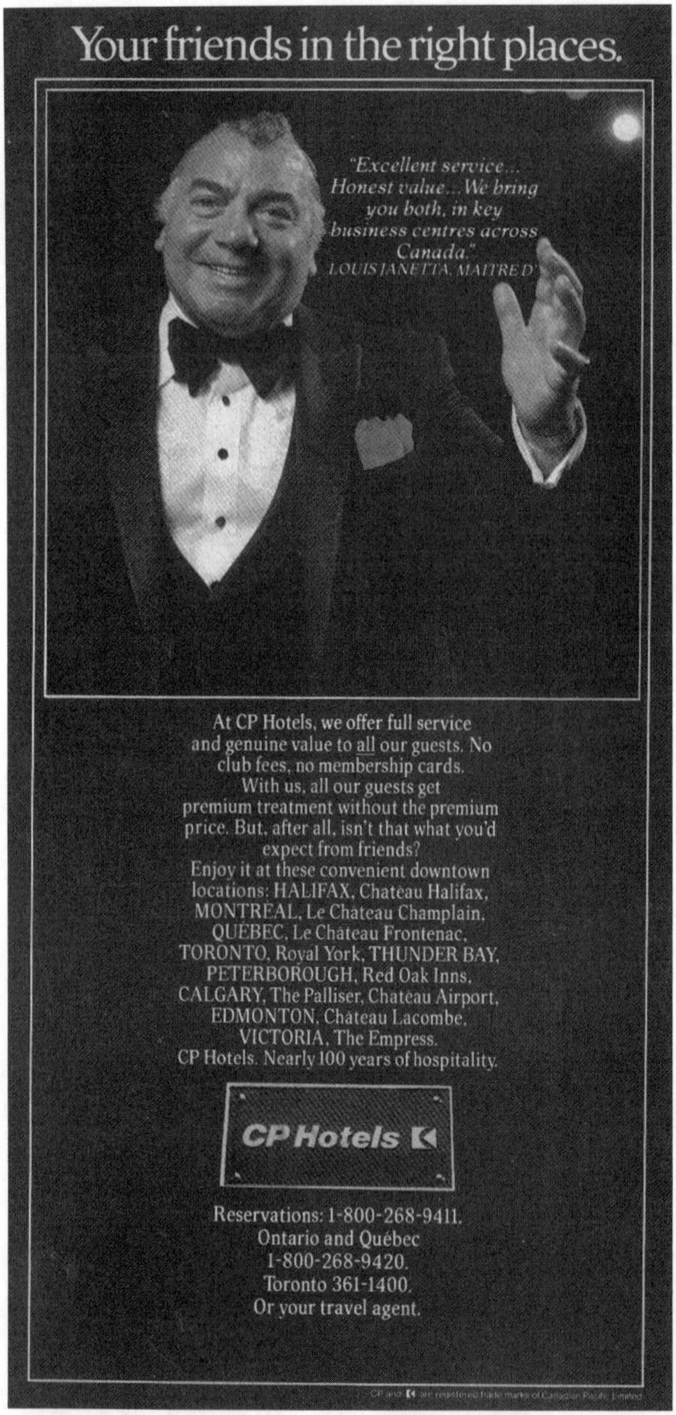

Louis in Rome

Louis in Rome

Louis & Corinne Jannetta

First trip back to Italy

A tiger & Louis - hamming it up at the Chin Picnic Media launch

The Bakers:
Patti, Dave, Ashley & Michelle

Chapter Four
Where the Stars Shone

In the early seventies, business at the Imperial Room was off a little bit, but our strategy of bringing in big-name stars was generally working well. The numbers were down, but we were still making enough money to pay for the advertising and marketing and we were still drawing guests to the hotel for extended stays from as far away as Philadelphia when we had stars they wanted to see. But the people at the head office in Montreal suddenly came up with what they thought was a brilliant idea. The Cafe Conc at the Chateau Champlain Hotel in that city had had great success with a revue called Follies Royale, produced by an impresario, Tibor Rootis, who had also made something of a name for himself with productions in the Bahamas.

Gordon Cardy, our new general manager, had no choice but to agree with Mr. Picard, the chairman of the Canadian Pacific board, that the Royal York should present the Follies too. After all, the show wasn't as expensive as the artists we had been bringing in and it had already proven itself a winner. But the Chateau Champlain booked a lot of conventions and other functions and the show was included in the package, so naturally it was successful.

I was appalled. I had meetings with Mr. Cardy and the food and beverage manager, Frank Bilecki, bringing it to their attention again and again that the Imperial Room was a showcase for the stars. Our audience, the people who had seen how great our stars were and who had supported us for years, wouldn't come to see a revue, especially one that featured scantily-clad dancers as the Follies did. That may have been fine in Montreal, but Montreal was a very different city from Toronto.

My objections fell on deaf ears. At the time, there wasn't a separate hotel unit in the Canadian Pacific family, and when word came down from the CP board, that word was law. When Mr. Picard came to Toronto on business, I even accosted him in the Black Knight Room and, very upset, told him this show was not for the Imperial Room. But I guess they made us an offer we ultimately couldn't refuse. The Follies were forced upon us.

In the fall of 1971, the management spent $30,000 building a new stage for the revue. The group came down from Montreal for four weeks of rehearsal. The Follies featured singers, dancers, and comedians, as well as some vaudeville-type acts. In Montreal, they had some fairly good local names sprucing up the shows. I didn't doubt that Tibor was a successful show producer (he eventually produced The Three Tenors programs with Pavarotti, Domingo, and Carreras around the world), but I didn't think he had a feel for what the Toronto audience wanted or would accept. I was certain he didn't know what the audience for the Imperial Room -- now one of the greatest rooms in North America and the only game in town -- really appreciated.

My view was confirmed a few days before the Follies opened. Right on the steps by the door of the Imperial Room, Tibor grinned at me and said, "We're going to get rid of all the snobs."

I felt like punching him right in the nose. I said, "Snobs? You're talking about people who come here two or three times a week, who have their weddings and anniversaries here, who bring their out-of-town guests here. This is like their second home." I didn't mention that many of the "snobs" were from the finest families in Toronto, classy people who were good to everyone, and people I had known since I was a busboy and waiter in the 1940's.

Just before opening, I had meetings with all the Imperial Room people. Mr. Cardy asked me to also speak to the staff of the whole hotel. He told me to tell them about the show and how great it was going to be and for them to make sure they told all the guests how wonderful it was. I didn't believe a word of it, but we were all still working for the Royal York Hotel and had to do our best to make it a success. It was booked for a six-month run.

We opened up to a fairly substantial crowd, all by invitation. After the show's premier, about thirty to forty people showed up on any given night. It was a total disaster. Some of the show wasn't bad. Some of it was terrible. A couple of acts were in what I thought was extremely bad taste, and we ended up buying out some acts that were just too awful to keep. We advertised like crazy, but the marketing didn't bring anyone in.

Around the same time, the corporation was reorganized and Don Curtis became the head of a new and separate hotel organization. He saw the wisdom of going beyond even what we had accomplished in the previous decade. He gave us the financial leeway to begin bringing in some of the greatest stars in the world. For the next decade and more, the Imperial Room was among the very finest nightclubs in the world, a place where the brightest stars could really shine.

Marlene Dietrich

As the Imperial Room was emerging from the Follies Royale disaster in 1974, we needed a truly major star to establish a new standard for excellence and set a new tone for the room. I believed, along with Gordon Cardy, the people of Toronto wanted the best and were ready to pay for it. To begin the new regime, we needed someone the public would recognize immediately as one of the very best in the world. We decided on a legend: Marlene Dietrich.

Already in her seventies, the great Dietrich was still appearing frequently, though by that time usually in theaters or concert halls rather than night clubs. But her name and celebrity had been linked with clubs ever since her performance as Lola Lola in the 1931 German film, "The Blue Angel," had made her a star around the world. She had performed in cabarets all over the globe in the fifties and sixties after her movie career slowed down. We felt the Imperial Room was a perfect venue for her unique talents.

For me, this was a dream come true, and not just because the phone never stopped ringing for reservations once her name was announced. I had seen all her movies in the thirties and forties, many of them several times. She was a great actress and I respected her. I loved seeing her on the screen. Looking at her face, she was not beautiful, but there was something unique and very special about her. That's what made her a star. I was really looking forward to meeting her.

I arrived at the room late on her opening day. I was sad to see that reality didn't meet my expectations. She was very upset with her manager, Michael Benedict, about something that was bothering her. She was yelling and screaming and abusing the poor fellow. She didn't impress me much. I thought, "What a rude woman, embarrassing her manager in front of the staff at rehearsal. What a terrible person."

By this time, I'd known many great acts. I was there as a protector. I was always backstage, tending to their needs, making sure their room was always first class, comforting them when needed. But when suddenly confronted with such a very rude individual, I thought, "Who needs it?" I didn't even want to go backstage, other than to escort her to the stage, as I always did with our artists.

My mood improved on opening night when I could feel the genuine excitement in the room, anticipating her entrance. Her road manager brought her down from her suite to her dressing room in a wheelchair. I pushed her up a ramp to the stage that we had built for the occasion.

Wearing a long, beaded gown, she walked through the curtain and held on to a rail to make her way to the microphone. No one could see the cast on her injured leg. She was thin and frail, but just standing there in a soft mauve spotlight, she worked a wonderful magic. She was elegant, glamorous, and ageless, just as I always believed the Imperial Room itself to be. The crowd's applause was deafening. She was never a great chanteuse, but once she started singing in that distinctive deep voice of hers, everyone was mesmerized. Everyone loved her. She became what I had felt her to be for decades -- one of the greatest stars God ever created.

The week went smoothly. During the time she was there, I came to especially admire her courage in going out every night despite what I'm sure must have been a great deal of pain, performing magnificently to an always sold-out room. But what you see onstage is not what you see backstage. She was aloof and kind of cold, always keeping to herself. She never wanted to see anyone in her dressing room. I was about the only person allowed backstage. Her dressing room was considered off limits.

After the first couple of nights, I felt more comfortable and knocked on her dressing room door. I couldn't help myself. The star-struck fan came out. I had to tell her how much I loved her 1936 movie, "The Garden of Allah," a film I'd seen so many times in my youth. It was a wonderful technicolor movie about a defrocked priest who fell in love with her and ran away from the church. I simply had to tell her that I'd had the privilege and pleasure of speaking with her three co-stars from that film. I told her how excited I had been, at age fourteen, meeting C. Aubrey Smith in the Venetian Room. I told her about serving Charles Boyer, who had played the priest, and the great Basil Rathbone. When I told her that, her icy exterior seemed to melt. She smiled, embraced me, kissed both my cheeks, and promised she would come back to the Imperial Room. When her run was over, she left me some caricatures plus a picture signed affectionately "To Luciano."

Marlene kept her promise, coming back the next year, in 1975. This time, things didn't go so well. At rehearsal, she decided she didn't like the sound system and demanded it be replaced. We scrambled to get some sound engineers working in time for her opening that very night. At show time, she made a dramatic entrance. She opened her mouth to sing and nothing came out. The sound man had plugged the new sound system into the socket at my desk. When I shut off the house lights, the sound system shut down too. I was at my table and rushed back to my desk and switched to a different system. The incident didn't make her very happy.

Worse, Frank Rasky, not the greatest newspaper critic in the world, was in the audience that night. He wrote a review that said terrible things about her. He wrote about her wearing too much make-up and having a waxy face. He criticized her for not speaking much with the audience and disparaged her singing in what I thought was a nasty way. I was very upset with Frank. Why harass someone at her advanced age when she's still filling the room?

I visited her a lot backstage during the engagement, and I know she was deeply wounded by that review. She said, "Why would he say those things? I can't sing. All my life I can't sing. I am an actress. I interpret songs."

People started canceling their reservations. It was a disaster for the room, especially since we had invested $50,000 in her for the week, much more than we usually paid artists at that time.

The run ended badly too. All week, Yul Brynner, who was performing in a play at the Royal Alex, had been trying to see her. They had had a relationship some years earlier, which I guess must have ended badly. She refused to see him. I never found out the details, but I knew that Marlene could hold a grudge. Guy Lombardo had told me a story that showed just how long she could hold one. Guy said that way back in the early thirties his orchestra was playing the Coconut Grove in Hollywood. In the audience were Marlene, Carole Lombard, and Russ Columbo, a man with a beautiful voice rivaling Bing Croby's who became known as "Hollywood's tragic crooner" when he was killed by a ricocheting bullet. They invited Guy to Palm Springs to party with them, but he'd been touring and was tired and wanted to go home to his wife, so he declined, which seemed to offend Marlene. Forty years later, he was doing a television show with her and she still wouldn't talk to him. She never forgave him for not going to Palm Springs.

For her final late show on Saturday night, Yul was in the audience. After each song he was on his feet, applauding and shouting, "Bravo." He had even sent a peace offering of four dozen roses. Unfortunately, they were left outside the room. One of the hotel staff, a girl whose boyfriend had just died, thought they had been discarded and took them home to make herself feel better. They were replaced by other flowers, but four dozen roses are hard to come by after midnight on a Saturday night. Yul tried to get backstage. Marlene would not see him.

Sadly, this engagement was one of the last, if not the last, nightclub performance she ever gave. She fell again at a show soon after, possibly influenced by her long-standing bouts with alcohol. This time she broke her leg, a compound fracture. She retired from the club and cabaret circuit. After making one last movie in 1978, she spent the last ten years of her life bedridden in seclusion in Paris.

For all her faults and idiosyncrasies, to this day I am very proud to have known her. I loved her. She was in a class by herself and brought a great and unmatched presence to the Imperial Room.

First Ladies of Song

I admit to a bias toward the songs and voices of Italian men. How could I not? But I've admired and loved many female vocalists over the years. When I think back on all the singers I've heard, seen, and known, there are only two I would grace with the term "first ladies of song." One, of course, who was widely known by that title -- Ella Fitzgerald. But to my mind, another singer had a career that put her at the same level.

Lena Horne

I first met the one and only Lena Horne when she was on tour with Tony Bennett in the 1970's. The two of them performed at the O'Keefe Centre in Toronto and Tony introduced us. She was fabulous on stage and just as enchanting on a personal level. She was in a class by herself.

I had thought highly of her talents since the 1940's. I wasn't really aware of her early days as a dancer in the chorus line at the Cotton Club in New York, but when she started making movies, I couldn't help but notice, especially when she gave such a bravura performance in "Stormy Weather." The color barrier in Hollywood and in America generally in those days kept her from reaching her full potential as an actress, but I followed her career avidly as she made great recordings and worked the big nightclubs. I still treasure her 1957 album, "Lena Horne at the Waldorf Astoria."

I always wanted to book her at the Imperial Room, but she had retreated from public life in the early 1970's after a series of personal tragedies. When she returned at the end of that decade, I was thrilled we could get her to come. After her two appearances at the room, in October 1979 and January 1981, she made a big comeback on Broadway in a one-woman show, "Lena Horne: The Lady and Her Music."

She had such a timeless quality to her. She was about 65 years old when she first appeared with us. She was elegant and stylish and glamorous and still had the powerful voice she'd used to captivate audiences for decades. If I had any problem with her performances, it was that in conversation with the audience she went on a little too long about the injustices she'd suffered in Hollywood, especially when Ava Gardner was chosen over her to play the mixed-blood heroine of "Showboat." I had read somewhere that she had gotten over her bitterness from that period, though you'd never know it from the way she spoke. But that was a minor transgression in my view. She filled the room every night. We were always sold out.

After her last performance, I sent one of my captains, Joseph, to her dressing room with a bottle of champagne. He came back and told me Lena wanted to see me. There must have been 200 people hoping for autographs waiting in a line that snaked around from the main Imperial Room door all the way to the backstage area. I made my way through the crowd to find her alone with her manager and wardrobe lady. She said, "Louis, close the door and open the champagne. You're family." I thanked her for being so great and for being with us.

The next year she was in town for a one-woman show at the O'Keefe Centre and sent me front-row seats. I couldn't get to the theater before intermission. As the second half began, she looked down, saw me, smiled, and said, "Hey, Luciano." She was wonderful. She was one of a kind. She was family.

Ella Fitzgerald

Ella Fitzgerald holds a special place in my heart as well as at the top of my list of favorite artists and favorite people. I had been a fan of hers since the 1940's, even though I was never that much of a jazz fan. I always loved her voice and, while I appreciated her wordless virtuoso improvisations—her scat singing—I loved the way she got across the real meaning of the songs she sang, especially ballads. She was a storyteller and, without any doubt, one of the greatest stars of all time.

She first appeared at the Imperial Room in 1969, and I, along with everyone else who saw her, fell a little bit in love as soon as she started singing. Her voice was so captivating, her tone so clear, her style so rhythmic, her range so broad. She was sensational. Frank Sinatra said she was the best singer in the world, and who was I to disagree?

Off stage, we got to be good friends. Personally, she displayed the same kind of friendly cheerfulness she did in her singing. She always traveled with a woman who looked after her needs and a road manager, Tony Carvello. Both of them were fine people and it was a pleasure to work with them. Her manager, the legendary Norman Granz, was more difficult to deal with. He was very strict, a perfectionist who insisted that everything be absolutely perfect, which was understandable with a star of Ella's caliber. Thankfully, he usually only showed up for one of her opening nights.

Ella would occasionally come into the Imperial Room for a late lunch and I was always ready to have the kitchen prepare anything she wanted or, if we didn't have the right food, to have it quickly brought in from some other restaurant. But most of the time she kept to herself and stayed in her room to watch her beloved soap operas all day long. She would sometimes get testy if she had to miss her soaps.

Ella hated signing autographs, but was very giving in many other ways. Her manager didn't like it much, but when Gino Empry asked her to do charitable events, she was always agreeable. Almost every time she came to town, she would go out to the local chapter of Variety Village or do an afternoon show at the hotel for Toronto's underprivileged children.

We spent quite a bit of time together. Her image sometimes made people think that she was naïve or maybe not the smartest person in the world, but I found her to be very smart. She listened to music all the time and didn't talk all that much, but when she did she certainly seemed right on top of things.

Most performers need to get loose or unwind before going on stage, and I developed the habit over the years of helping them do it. Sometimes the need was great. Eartha Kitt, for example, was the most nervous person I ever met. Some nights it seemed she wouldn't be able to go on at all without a little calming down, so I'd join her in her dressing room and we'd talk and do a little dance. Ella wasn't the nervous type, but she appreciated me coming in to talk and do some physical exercises, always without her bending her knees. Sometimes I'd start to sing Italian songs and, to my delight, she would sing along with me.

Eventually, she wouldn't go on or off the stage unless I escorted her, though during one of her earliest engagements I had a nervous moment. I'd been standing by the wings yelling, "Bravo" as she finished her act. I took her hand to help her down the steps and she looked at me with flashing eyes and said, "Don't you 'boy' me."

"Miss Fitzgerald, what do you mean? I said, 'Bravo. Bravo.'"

"Oh, okay."

During her performance I'd often be having dinner at the back of the room. But Tony Carvello would come by to tell me she was waiting until I arrived to take her backstage. She would always wait for me.

She put on the most wonderful shows, always with a trio that traveled with her who would work with Howard Cable's orchestra, which she loved. All her accompanists were top flight musicians, especially whichever piano player she brought with her, sometimes the great jazz man, Jimmy Rowles, sometimes someone equally as talented. Audiences loved her, and everyone who was anyone in Toronto or even the country, from Prime Minister Pierre Trudeau on down, would come to see her shows.

She played the Imperial Room almost right to the end, until she stopped singing. With each of her eight appearances, it became more and more clear she was losing her eyesight and becoming very frail. Her health problems multiplied during the next few years, plagued as she was by heart disease and diabetes.

The last time I saw her, she was in town for a concert at Roy Thomson Hall and came to see Eddie Fisher, one of the last stars to appear with us. Eddie, unfortunately, wasn't that good and wasn't doing much business. But those who were at the Imperial Room that night probably never forgot the moment when Eddie came down off the stage to sing to her and she, delightfully, sang back. The way Eddie was singing, it may not have been the greatest duet in history, but it was a lovely and historic moment and one of my fondest memories.

Eddie Fisher with host Patti Wagner

Every Italian's a Singer

One of the great pleasures of being in the Imperial Room was that I got to know so many fine singers of Italian heritage, all of them influenced by Frank Sinatra, all of them making it big in the ten-year interlude between the big bands and rock 'n roll. In fact, it was great to be Italian in North America from the late forties right through to the mid-sixties. So many singers, so much music, such great songs.

I especially liked the Italian crooners because most got their start in talent shows (which always reminded me of my father's efforts in that direction) and because most had a long and hard road to the top (which reminded me of my own rise to a position of some prominence). Each made a name for himself, even if he had to change his name to do it.

We could never afford the chairman of the board himself, of course. He was way out of the league of any nightclub outside Las Vegas. But at least I did get to meet and spend some time with Frank Sinatra when he stayed at the Royal York during a tour in 1976 when he gave a concert at Maple Leaf Gardens. I greeted him at the door at three in the morning, stayed with him as he generously signed autographs for a fairly large group of aging ladies waiting in the lobby, then escorted him to his suite. I found him to be a very nice man. He gave me a picture signed "To Lewis." I got back to him and said, "Mr. Sinatra, I'm Italian, not Jewish." He gave me another one signed "To Louis."

We had Frank Sinatra Jr. at the Imperial Room a couple of times in the late 1970's, a booking I tried to avoid. But I got calls from his agent all the time, each one more insistent than the last. We finally signed him for around Easter time when things were usually slow. The first time around, he talked about his father a lot and gave a pretty good show. The second time, he didn't talk about his father. His voice was very pleasant.

Frank Sinatra Jr.

Frank Jr. never achieved the heights his dad did, but many of the other crooners we had over the years were almost as big as Sinatra in their time. I admired them all, though sometimes I had a little trouble with the way they behaved on stage.

Tony Bennett

As an Italian and as a wannabe singer, I always had the greatest respect for Tony Bennett. I remember seeing him at the Casino Theatre on Queen Street in Toronto when I was a kid. He was just a teenaged Anthony Benedetto himself then, but had already attracted some attention, especially among Italians, when he performed beside New York's Mayor Fiorello La Guardia at the opening of the Triborough Bridge in 1936. When he came to town in those early days, he came to my old stomping grounds—the district around St. Agnes Church where all the Italians lived—not to sing, but just to hang around and feel at home.

He made even more of an impression on me, as he did on so many others, in the early 1950's. He became a hit parade sensation with songs like "Because of You," "Rags to Riches," "Stranger in Paradise," and so many others. I loved them all. He had the greatest voice for popular standards I had ever heard, a lovely tenor that gradually deepened over the years. When rock 'n roll came in and he didn't get on the charts as often, I bought all his albums. I was never too much of a jazz fan, but I loved his work with Count Basie and other artists in the late fifties and early sixties.

It was just around the time I took over the Imperial Room that Tony made a big comeback on the pop charts with "I Left My Heart in San Francisco, the beautiful ballad that became his signature tune. I knew he was having a terrific career on the concert circuit and on recordings at the time, but I was so happy he had returned to the mainstream prominence I thought he deserved. Another Italian boy made good. I was even happier when he followed that up with hits like "I Wanna Be Around," "The Good Life," "Who Can I Turn To," and "If I Ruled the World."

We first had him at the Imperial Room in December 1971, and he inadvertently did me a great service. This was the time when my policy of booking the stars was under attack. We were then featuring the Follies Royale, the tacky show some people at Canadian Pacific's head office thought we should have after it had been a success at the Chateau Champlain. I had been arguing, supported by Gordon Cardy most of the time, that the Imperial Room was not for revues. But we didn't have any choice or any control in the matter. The Follies was dictated by Montreal.

Mr. Cardy had me making speeches about how great it was, but in fact, it was a disaster. All through the "star years" of the late 1960's, we'd had 800 people a night for two shows for the top acts. With the Follies, we'd dropped to about 40 people a night, tops.

Concetta & Frank Jannetta (my mother and father), Tony Bennett and Louis

When Tony Bennett played for a week, we continued to have a few numbers from the Follies performed before he came on. Of course, he sold out the room. When he left, the audience went back to nothing and my policy had been vindicated. Hotel management saw the light. We bought out the contracts of some of the lesser acts we had scheduled and, after four or five months, we went back to the stars.

I had never met Tony before, but we got along right off the bat. He was charming, gracious, and the most thorough professional I had ever known. Working with his long-time pianist and arranger, Ralph Sharon, he was the epitome of class. He was the sort of artist the Imperial Room was designed for. Over the next fourteen years, we had him come back eleven times, more than any other artist.

He always did great business, even though he didn't have a recording contract at the time and wasn't putting out new albums. People remembered and loved him. With some of the other acts we had, I'd often have to go backstage to comfort them if the turn out wasn't up to their expectations. So many performers have such fragile egos. If the room wasn't full, I always had a story for them: the NHL playoffs are on; the World Series is on; the weather's bad; the marketing was poor. For Tony Bennett, there could have been a hurricane hitting the city and the place would still be filled.

We developed a good relationship right from that first engagement. On the last night, I organized an after-show party for him and the musicians, as I usually did for the best artists. At the time, management allowed me to do whatever I wanted to do, so I'd get a big executive suite and have carte blanche as far as catering was concerned.

Lauren Bacall was in Toronto, performing in "Applause" at the Royal Alex. I took her backstage to see Tony and invited her and her cast to the party too. The gathering went on into the wee hours, and at about five in the morning, Tony asked me for paper and a pen. I gave him a lovely pen Paul Anka had given me as a gift. As Tony started to draw, I went over to Lauren, a wonderful lady who had had quite a few drinks, and said, "Miss Bacall, I'd like to sing to you."

She looked up at me, laughed uproariously, and said, "Oh, great, another wop who wants to sing." I figured she was just kidding, though I found out later she was upset at the time because Frank Sinatra had dumped her after she had revealed in the press that they were about to marry. She may have been down on Italians, but I think I surprised her by singing an Irish song first, before breaking into "Torna A Surriento." I told her every Italian's a frustrated singer. By the time I was finished, Tony held out a lovely caricature of me that remains one of my most prized possessions.

That was when I first learned about Tony's other life as an artist. I didn't know that from the time he began drawing chalk pictures on the sidewalks of Queens when he was five, Tony was an extraordinarily gifted and dedicated visual artist. He'd studied art as well as music. He'd worked in oils and watercolors, experimented with all kinds of subjects and styles, and exhibited his paintings all over the world under his family name, Anthony Benedetto.

Rocco & Gordon Cappuccitti with Tony Bennett

He always seemed to find time to paint every day, either from his hotel window or on his travels around whatever city he was playing. He liked a particular view from the Royal York and always asked for the same suite every time he came. He also delighted in visiting museums and galleries during his tours. He'd sometimes ask me, "What are you doing this afternoon?" If I was free, we'd get in his limo and tour galleries so he could buy art that he felt showed the same joy in creating beauty he so obviously felt himself. These trips were both a pleasure and an education for me.

A big stock promoter in town (I'll just call him Dave) was a regular patron, often coming in with a party of forty or fifty, and usually a classy guy. He was a great supporter of the Imperial Room and he loved Tony Bennett. He and his girlfriend, both dressed to the nines, came to see Tony. The first show went well and Dave told me he wanted to stay for the second one, but he had to be up front. He slipped me a $50 bill to help me make the arrangements. I had a waiter put another table right next to the stage, which I generally didn't do. But the people from the first show were already gone, so I didn't foresee any problem.

Almost as soon as Tony started his second show, Dave, a big six-foot-six guy, stood up and started singing "I Left My Heart in San Francisco." I thought, "Oh my God." As Tony moved to the far side of the stage with the spotlight following him, I rushed over from my table and said, "Dave. Dave. Emergency. Your mother's on the phone." He followed me out the door and I never let him back in.

Tony stood head and shoulders above every other artist I met in so many ways. In the mid-1970's, he performed at Hamilton Place, not far from Toronto. I took twenty-four of my friends to the matinee. After the performance, I asked if he would join us for dinner at the Royal Connaught Hotel. He left his limo waiting and came in our little car. As we walked into the restaurant, the whole place started to applaud. There was a great big chair at the head of the long table, and I gestured for Tony to take this place of honor. He refused, saying, "No, you sit there." He sat on my right. He left at six o'clock to get ready for his second performance. My group stayed, had liqueurs and coffee, and asked for the bill. No bill. Tony had picked up the tab for twenty-four people. No one had ever done anything like that in my experience. Most celebrities never put their hand in their own pocket.

He did so many wonderful things for me over the years. He smoothed out a problem I had one night with Don Curtis, the chairman of CP Hotels, changing Curtis from an antagonist to one of my biggest fans. He stayed an extra night to present an award at a banquet for my hockey league. He came to the rink to drop the opening puck early on a Sunday morning, watched the game, then came to my house to spend the day, making me a real big shot to my neighbors who all milled around. In some cities where he was playing, people would tell him they were friends of mine and he'd pick up their tab. His generosity extended to my staff. In all my years at the Royal York, he was the only star to invite my waiters to lunch, showing his appreciation for the role they played in making his bookings a success.

He has gone out of his way to give special treatment to Corinne and me and my friends wherever and whenever we met. One time in Fort Lauderdale, I, along with about half a dozen people from my condo building, headed down to a gallery where he was showing his art. The deal was that anyone who bought a $50 Benedetto print would have it autographed. We stood in line with the other "Friends of Tony." As soon as he saw me, he stopped everything, took us all out of line, signed autographs for all of us, and gave me a special print to hang in the restaurant I'd recently opened in Toronto. To the people in my entire condo building, I was a star in my own right after that. They couldn't do enough for me.

Louis with wife Corrine and Tony Bennett

Another time, he was showing his paintings while performing during Italian Week in Boca Raton, Florida. I didn't see his show, but we enjoyed a wonderful dinner in a terrific restaurant that was actually closed, but not to Tony Bennett. I especially enjoyed the get-together because we were joined by a retired Maitre D' who had worked at the Copa Cabana when Tony sang there. Any opportunity to trade war stories with your peers is to be treasured.

More recently, in the late 1990's, I went to Florida at the end of February. A friend of mine, who looked after my condo, picked me up and said, "I hear your buddy, Tony, is playing in Fort Lauderdale. Do you think you can do something? Susie will go crazy." (Susie was his wife.)

The concert was sold out, of course, but I got hold of the Fort Lauderdale Center of the Performing Arts and asked when the sound check was going to be. My friend and I went down to the stage entrance. The first limo to show up at three in the afternoon brought Tony's road manager, Vance Anderson, who emerged and said, "Louis, what are you doing here?"

"Trying to get tickets, but they're all gone." Vance said that probably nothing could be done, but told me Tony would be arriving in an hour and to just stay around. When Tony arrived, he greeted me warmly and took me and my buddy, also named Tony, inside the theatre, one of the most beautiful theatres I'd ever seen. He let me take a picture of the two Tony's with the theatre in the background and said, "After the sound check, we'll go for dinner. How about tonight? You looked after?"

I said, "I just arrived and didn't know you were here. You're sold out."

"Vance, you can put two chairs on the stage, can't you?"

"Whatever you say, Tony."

I said, "I don't want to take advantage of you, but I'd really appreciate it if I could bring his wife and daughter to the show. They love you so much."

"Vance, get some other chairs. And make sure you come backstage, Louis. I'd like you to meet my brother."

He gave an unbelievable performance that night. The show was great. I had to agree with the local newspaper the next day when it said that with Sinatra and Mel Torme gone, "Tony Bennett is the last living American monument."

Now, early in the 21st century, Tony is bigger and better than ever. It's hard to believe that he's been in the business for more than sixty years, but he only ages like a fine wine. He probably got more critical acclaim in the late 1990's than he ever had in his career, and that's saying something. I saw him perform at Roy Thomson Hall in Toronto in 2004, where he put aside front-row seats for me and some guests and introduced me to the audience, something he's often done (and did again the next year in Niagara Falls). He sang "O Sole Mio" and told the crowd, "This is for Mr. Jannetta." To me, he had never sounded better. I often had the pleasure of his company at Jannetta's, the restaurant I opened in the 1990's. I tried to make it a sanctuary for him, a place where he could relax and enjoy my pasta—he loves my pasta—and we could talk into the night about anything and everything, including the glory days of the Imperial Room, the good times and the bad. I always tried to make things first class for him. I think that was the essence of our special relationship.

TONY BENNETT — Singing his way back to Toronto.

IMPERIAL MEMORIES

His kind of town

SYLVIA TRAIN

HE LIKES US, HE LIKES US: Tony Bennett plays the grandest venues in the world, but he still misses the Imperial Room.

"It was the best on the North American continent," said Bennett on the phone from New York. "The only room coming close is the Waldorf's Empire Room. But they don't have Louis Janetta!"

Now he's coming to Toronto to play Ontario Place Saturday, Aug. 5 for two shows (5 p.m., 8:30 p.m.)

Bennett is in an enviable position. He makes his living doing what he loves: Singing and painting. Of his 91 albums, his latest, *Astoria*, is named after the town where he was born more than 60 years ago to a Queens, N.Y., grocer and seamstress.

"That's where the blue-collar workers come from, the people who make New York City work. It's also where columnist Jimmy Breslin was brought up."

This year, he's had 31 exhibitions of his art. "All in good galleries," said Bennett proudly. He signs them with his real name, Anthony Benedetto.

He's been single since his divorce more than 10 years ago. "I'm just going along, raising my grandchildren and children."

His two sons, Danny and Daegal, take care of the business side of his two professions, and manage his career. And because of them, life has become much simpler.

His two daughters, 15 and 19, are interested in theatre and are attending the Lee Strasberg school. Bennett's home is in New York, and though his daughters live in L.A., they spend a lot of time with him in the Big Apple.

He's going to Japan in November and then will play concerts in England and Europe.

"I heard Ed Mirvish is going to open a supper club," said Bennett. "I hope he calls on me — he's such a great guy."

I'm told that there is interest in leasing space in a building owned by Mirvish for that purpose. Nothing has been finalized as yet. I'll keep you posted, folks.

Retirement age is coming up quickly but Bennett doesn't have any intention of slowing down. "I'd like to just keep on going."

* * *

CHIPPER DALE: Jennifer Dale is busy these days. She just finished shooting the TV movie *Blood Sport*, with Ian McShane and Patrick Macnee for CTV and U.S. syndication. Harvey Hart directs. She is also a regular on CBC's *In Opposition*, a sitcom co-starring Kathy Laskey ... Jackie Burroughs is starring in the *Road To Avonlea*, the CBC-Walt Disney series produced by Kevin Sullivan.

* * *

GETTING IN HER LICKS: Marianne Heller, who brainstormed the Festival Village for the Festival Of Festivals, has come up with another terrific idea. She's importing American Glace, the ice cream that's a smash lick in the U.S. It has only 46 calories per serving, it's cholesterol-free and has no artificial ingredients. I bought a cone at 102 Cumberland and it tasted terrific.

* * *

MORE SECRETS: Sunrise Films' successful series *My Secret Identity* starts shooting again Monday with regulars Jerry O'Connell and Derek McGrath. They'll do 24 more of the shows, which air on CTV Thursdays at 7:30, and are syndicated in the U.S.

One night at Jannetta's, I even let go of a little secret I'd kept for years. One of the very few times Tony was ever sharp with me came when Dave, the man who had stayed for his second performance and loudly started singing "I Left My Heart In San Francisco" as Tony started his show. Afterwards, he was quite upset.

I said, "Tony, I don't know whether you remember the night this guy started to sing and I rushed down to get him out of there. It was the first time you were ever upset with me and you said, 'What did he do, give you $50 for the table?' I've got to confess. He did give me a fifty-dollar bill." We both laughed at the memory.

As we parted during a recent visit to Toronto, he put his arms around me and said, "Louis, thank you so much for your great friendship." My friendship? When he was the one who did so much for me? He was the star everyone idolized and who made me a hero to many. Without him the Imperial Room would have been empty long ago.

What always impressed me was that he stayed true to himself all those years, singing great songs in his unique and great way, whatever the popular taste of the day. His passion and love of music and performing and making great art have been inspiring. Having the opportunity to know him personally has been one of the great joys of my life.

Frankie Laine

One of our earliest headliners in the mid-1960's was Frankie Laine, or Francis Lo Vecchio as he was known when he was born in 1913. He grew up in Chicago's Little Italy, the son of Sicilian immigrants. His father was a barber who cut Al Capone's hair. I got a kick out of Frankie's early background—car salesman, bouncer, singing waiter, marathon dance champion, plant worker. He had a big moment in Los Angeles in the forties when he rescued a kid drowning in a swimming pool. The kid turned out to be Perry Como's son. He had an even bigger moment when Hoagy Carmichael heard him sing "Old Rocking Chair" in a Hollywood club.

It wasn't long after that that I and everybody else discovered him when he recorded great songs like "That's My Desire," "Mule Train," "Jezebel," "I Believe," "Jealousy," and dozens of others. Frankie never sang many Italian songs and country and/or western music has never been a favorite of mine, but it was hard not to like his renditions of the theme songs from western movies like "High Noon," "Man With A Star," and "Gunfight At The OK Corral," as well as the "Rawhide" TV theme.

After he dropped off the hit-parade charts, he had a good career in concerts and cabarets. My wife and I first saw him perform in Buffalo, and got to know him a bit at the same time. When we booked him at the Imperial Room, I knew he still had lots of fans who remembered his records and TV appearances (he had his own variety series in the 1950's). But I was surprised at how many fans he had. He was always in demand and almost always sold out.

We had him on several occasions, and every time Frankie and I would share a glass of wine or two backstage and talk. He was a versatile singer and a charming man who had wonderful stories about the many fascinating people he'd worked with during his long career. My only concern was that, as he got older, he'd talk to the audience more than he would sing. But he always remained a popular favorite and a personal favorite of mine. For years I always received a Christmas card from him.

Julius LaRosa

By the time Julius LaRosa appeared at the Imperial Room in the 1960's, his name recognition was wearing a little thin. But he still had a following, mainly of older people who still remembered the event that marked his career even more than his singing.

Julius was a Brooklyn boy and one of the few Italian singers of his era who kept his own name and never forgot his roots. He sang with the American Navy Band, then as soon as he got out of the service, went right onto "Arthur Godfrey and His Friends," one of the most popular shows in the early days of television.

He lasted almost two years until one of the most famous incidents of TV lore happened. He finished singing "Manhattan" when Arthur came over and said, "Thank you, Julius. And that, folks, was Julius' swan song." Getting fired on the air surprised the hell out of Julius and all the viewers too. Supposedly, he was fired for "lack of humility," but he had really just become too independent. While I had a good relationship with Arthur in later years, and he had a Mr. Nice Guy public image as the "King of Television," behind the scenes he apparently was autocratic, if not just plain mean and tyrannical.

Unfortunately for Arthur, the public saw the firing as the big guy dumping on the little guy, and his career started going downhill. Julius survived with a couple of his own TV series and a turn on Broadway that was pretty well received, but his career was always a bit iffy.

I liked his stuff. He had a casual and direct way of singing. He could tell a story, so he liked ballads and so did his audience. I especially liked his Italian songs, of course. His first hit, "Anywhere I Wander," was okay, but "Eh, Cumpari," which came out right around the time of his firing, was terrific. It became an Italian tradition. He followed that up with "Domani," another favorite.

He was a nice man and easy to get along with. He gave a pretty good show and did okay as far as audience turnout went. He was different from other stars in that he liked to keep the lights on during his show. He thought it helped him make the eye contact he needed. Even after being in the business for so long, however, it seemed to me like he was still learning his job. He went right into the navy after high school, so he didn't have the kind of club and other experience so many other singers used to sharpen their performances. He didn't seem as polished as he might be after so many years in the business.

One night during his run after I had already gone home after the first show, I got a call to come back as soon as I could. Something had offended Julius and right in the middle of his act, he had walked off stage. To this day, I don't know what it was that bothered him so much.

Jerry Vale

Jerry Vale was another New Yorker, Genaro Vitaliano from the Bronx. He started singing for customers when he was a shoeshine boy at age eleven and later won a talent contest at the Club del Rio, quite a famous outfit at the time, at least among Italians.

Like Julius LaRosa, his big hits started coming in the early and mid-1950's, with songs like "You Can Never Give Me Back My Heart," "I Live Each Day," "Innamorata," and "You Don't Know Me," his biggest hit. He became a personal favorite in the early sixties after he finally convinced his record company to let him record whole albums of Italian songs like "Innamorata," "Volare," "Amore," "Scusami," "Arrivederci, Roma," and "Al Di La," his signature tune. He was just about the only popular crooner of the times so devoted to the Italian repertoire.

He was a wonderful singer with a beautiful high-tenor voice, and he kept his audience after he disappeared from the charts with many albums and many appearances on television and in clubs all through the fifties, sixties, and seventies. In fact, he was still going strong into the 21st century.

We had him at the Imperial Room in 1973. He gave really good performances, but after the show, he'd sit on the edge of the stage and start talking to people. That was fair enough, but they would often have requests. He'd sing some -- sometimes not all that well -- and to my mind would lose the audience. Everything he did on stage earlier in the evening would be forgotten, and he'd leave the stragglers with a poor impression. I could never understand that. He should have just gotten off the stage. As Tony Bennett always told me, "Let them keep applauding. Leave them wanting more."

Al Martino and Lorenzo Grella

Al Martino came to the Imperial Room in the fall of 1971, another great singer I was proud to showcase. He had a look and a style and a way about him that certainly hinted at his beginnings as the son of Italian immigrants in Philadelphia, a guy who worked as a bricklayer in his dad's construction business before becoming a singer. Mario Lanza, a hero of mine and a Cini family friend (Al was born Alfred Cini), encouraged him. Once he won first place on Arthur Godfrey's Talent Scouts radio program, his first record, "Here In My Heart," sold a million copies.

It took almost another 15 years for him to score a second million-seller—"Spanish Eyes" in 1965—but in between he had quite a few lesser hits, mostly ballads. I liked most of his work, especially a song he recorded later in his career, "To The Door Of The Sun" (which was really "Alle Porte Del Sole"). He had a certain confidence in his delivery I enjoyed.

He did well at the room. While he was there, I invited him to my house for dinner. My mother made him one of her special pasta dishes with meatballs. During this visit, he seemed more interested in phoning Los Angeles and listening to my collection of Al Martino albums than talking with my family. But we got along pretty well as his run at the hotel went on.

I was glad we had him in 1971 and not later. The next year, he played Johnny Fontane in Frances Ford Coppola's film "The Godfather," more or less portraying Frank Sinatra as he tried to land a role in "From Here to Eternity."

Al did a nice job as far as the acting went. In the movie he sang a great Italian number, "O Marenariello" ("I Have But One Heart"). He also did well with his recording of the film's love theme, "Speak Softly Love." But after playing that role, Al wasn't too well accepted by the Italian community.

Al rolled with the punches. Even during Grey Cup week, when the hotel was full of noisy revellers, he still kept on performing.

James Darren

Like Al Martino, James Darren came out of Philadelphia's Little Italy. James Ercolani only had a short career as a rock singer. He was a handsome guy and made more of a mark as an actor in movies such as "The Guns Of Navarone" and "Because They're Young." Even his career as a singer had more to do with playing the boyfriend in the Gidget movies in the late 50's and early 60's than with top-40 or album works. Those weren't exactly my kinds of movies. I never saw them. But I liked his voice in the half-dozen or so hits he had.

He put on good shows at the Imperial Room in 1977 and 1978. I think most of the audience came because they remembered "Gidget" or liked him in the "Time Tunnel" TV series. James was a very pleasant guy. One of my hockey players, Vic Tomasicchio, took him to Portofino, my favorite Italian restaurant in Toronto. During his stay, he got to know quite a few of my friends, all of them proud to have met him when he came back to prominence in the 1980's as one of the stars of "T. J. Hooker."

Victor Tomasicchio, Frank Mahavolich & Louis

Frankie Avalon

The last of the Philadelphia Italians to appear at the Imperial Room was Francis Avallone, better known as Frankie Avalon. He got his start on talent shows, too, though not on Arthur Godfrey's. He broke in by winning contests as a trumpet player then showing up as an uninvited performer at a party for Al Martino in 1952 after Al signed a new recording contract. He was only 12 at the time, but a talent scout noticed.

He really made it as a teen idol in the late fifties after appearing on "American Bandstand." I can't say that his material registered with me at the time. "De De Dinah" was a piece of bouncy fluff even Frankie hated. I didn't think much of his next few hits either, but then I wasn't a teenage girl. His hit-parade songs stopped in the early sixties but he kept a profile in the "Beach Party-Beach Blanket Bingo" series of movies. It was pretty much a nostalgia crowd that came to see him in Toronto in 1976.

He was very nice guy and put on a good show, though at one point he turned his back on the audience. This was always a pet peeve of mine. I generally kept my observations about performers to myself, but I thought I could say something if I knew the performer well enough, especially if they were Italian. Italians would listen. So I talked to him about it. He seemed grateful for the advice. At least, I know he didn't hold it against me. In later years, whenever he was in Toronto for other things, he would always come over to the Royal York to see me and say hello.

Vic Damone

Except for Tony Bennett, Vic Damone was the best of all the Italian singers of the era. That wasn't just my view. Frank Sinatra himself had once said, "If I had one wish, it would be for Vic Damone's tonsils. Vic has the best pipes in the business." He was a natural.

He was born Vito Farinola in Brooklyn and worked as an usher at the famous Paramount Theater in Times Square when he was still in high school. Part of his own legend is that while filling in as an elevator operator at the Paramount, he had Perry Como in the car. He stopped between floors, sang, and asked Perry if he had any talent. Perry said yes. Soon after, Vic won first prize on "Arthur Godfrey's Talent Scouts" show in 1945, recorded a couple of hits, then got his own radio program. I became aware of him in the late forties when he first had hits like "I Have But One Heart" and his duet with Patti Page, "Say Something Sweet to Your Sweetheart." He had a good, strong baritone voice I found very smooth and very appealing. He had a way with phrasing some other singers lacked. I liked some of his movies in the fifties, too, though only "Kismet" seemed to me to have any staying power. Most of his other hit records in the fifties were just so-so to me, but I liked "Tzena, Tzena, Tzena," "Ebb Tide," and "On the Street Where You Live."

By the time he first came to the Imperial Room in 1973, he'd had a long second (or maybe third) career as a performer on the nightclub and casino circuit. He was a regular in Las Vegas and became almost a regular in Toronto. He was fantastic, so much so we brought him back four more times. He could really move an audience, especially the women, who loved his romantic ballads. To them, he was still the heartthrob he was in his glory days. Me, I waited for the Italian stuff.

Vic was a great singer, but I thought his stage personality could have been a bit better. He put on a great show, but he always seemed to have a problem he mentioned to the audience during the act. He had a cold, he was tired, he was this, he was that. I never liked that in a performer. Then, during one show, he was singing a great song, "MacArthur Park," and just before he hit the height of the song, he turned his back on the audience. The greatest stars never do that. I didn't want to approach him directly about it, so I mentioned my concern to his musical director. He said, "I know, but I'm afraid to say anything to him."

That particular night, Frank Sinatra was giving a concert at Maple Leaf Gardens. Sinatra was Vic's idol, so I called my friend, Harold Ballard, the Gardens' owner, and arranged for front-row tickets. I had a limousine waiting outside to take us up to the Gardens after Vic's show. On the way to the concert, I bit the bullet and spoke to him about "MacArthur Park." It was a mild chiding, but he accepted it. A lot of other stars with bigger egos would have thrown such a presumptuous Maitre D' out of the limo. It probably didn't hurt our relationship that we had such great seats and that Sinatra gave him a lovely introduction to the Gardens crowd. (Frank loved Vic, who had been offered and, fortunately, turned down the role in "The Godfather" that Al Martino played.)

I always went out of my way to help Vic any way I could. During one of his engagements, Elizabeth Taylor and Carol Burnett were in the city making a movie. Vic tried, without much luck, to get in touch with them to ask them to come see his show. One day I heard from one of my captains that the two of them were in the Acadian Room (formerly the Venetian Room) in the lower level of the hotel having lunch with their husbands. I went down and introduced myself. In what I thought was wonderful and classy gesture, Elizabeth Taylor stood up and introduced me to Carol and the two men. I informed them that Vic would be so happy if they could come. Unfortunately, they were shooting scenes that night and couldn't make it. But they both left a lasting impression on me.

During his many appearances, I got to know Vic well. We'd often stay up late at night and into the early hours of the morning, talking about anything and everything. I found him a pleasant, amiable companion. Not everybody shared that view. I used to get an earful from the fine singer, Anna Maria Alberghetti, who played the room in 1975. She was a great friend of his first wife, the actress Pier Angeli, who had made a name for herself in movies like "Someone Up There Likes Me" and had died of a drug overdose in 1971. Anna had no use for Vic whatsoever, apparently blaming him for Angeli's death, even though they'd been divorced since the 1950's. She never stopped dumping on him.

In 1974, he appeared just a couple of weeks after his second wife, and the mother of his three daughters, had committed suicide. That was a tough engagement for him. I tried to make his time at the hotel more pleasant any way I could. I always had parties for him, and did that time too. But our conversations into the night were somber, interrupted by our softly singing together in his room.

On a more upbeat note, I took Vic to meet Lou Myles, one of the best tailors in the world and a master suit maker. Lou and I were kids together. He even worked as a busboy at the Royal York in 1942 or '43, but quit after a couple of days. He went into the fashion business in 1960 with the aim of making the world's most perfect suit. He succeeded. He made all my tuxedos and made garments for some of the most powerful and influential people, not only in Toronto but throughout North America—politicians, entertainers, businessmen, and sports stars. After that introduction, Lou made all Vic's tuxedos too, even if he had to fly them to wherever Vic was playing. For years afterward, Vic, Lou, and I would get together for dinner whenever Vic was in town.

His last appearance at the Imperial Room came in 1983, not all that long before the room closed up. After he married the actress and singer, Diahann Carroll, in 1987, the two of them toured together, putting on an excellent show at the O'Keefe Centre. As Vic's guest, I was given eight seats in front. During the show, he gave me a very kind and generous introduction to the audience. Then he said, "You know, ladies and gentlemen, with Mr. Jannetta here, I feel like I'm auditioning."

Luciano Pavarotti

As an Italian, I naturally absorbed opera as if it was mother's milk. The music of the greatest Italian composers was all around me in the neighborhood where I grew up and I remember attending a concert at Massey Hall in the early 1950's to hear Beniamino Gigli, the great successor of Enrico Caruso and the finest tenor in the world. Gigli's career took something of a beating after he became closely associated with Mussolini, but after the war, all was forgiven and he again toured the world. Since he stayed at the Royal York when he appeared in Toronto and dined at the Imperial Room, I had the opportunity to speak with him on many occasions. He was a delightful man.

I don't think I made it to another event at Massey Hall until Luciano Pavarotti appeared in concert in the 1970's. After the engagement was announced, I received a call from Georgina Maddot of the Pasquale family, which owned Unico products. The family had lived in Little Italy before becoming so important in the food industry, and I'd known Georgina since I was a busboy. As well as giving the concert, Pavarotti had agreed to sing at a ball at the Harbour Hilton Hotel to raise money for Villa Columbo, a Toronto home for elderly Italians. Georgina asked if I could do anything to help provide for the 1,200 guests expected at the ball. Fortunately, through my work at the Royal York and the Italian-Canadian Hockey League, I was able to call the president of Walker Distilleries, which donated all the wine, liquor, and liqueurs that were needed, and a senior executive at Labatt Breweries, which gave us all the beer. Corinne and I were invited to attend both the concert at Massey Hall and the ball, where we had wonderful seats at a table close to the dance floor.

After dinner, the guest of honor was introduced, and as he made his way to the stage along the dance floor, greeting the guests as he went, I approached him and said (in Italian), "Senore Pavarotti, my name is Luciano." I showed him my gold bracelet, which spells out "Luciano," and told him I had had the pleasure of knowing all the great opera stars who had come to perform in Toronto, especially my dear friend, Gigli.

He said, "Ah, Beniamino Gigli. The greatest."

I said, "I would be honored if you would accept my bracelet as a gift." He would not accept it, but he reached out his hand, grasped the back of my neck, and pulled me forward to kiss my forehead.

Several years later, he again came to Toronto, this time appearing at Maple Leaf Gardens, and again Georgina spoke to me about helping out with a fundraising ball, this time at the Royal York Hotel. I made all the arrangements, booked a room, and created a wonderful menu. But, unfortunately, Senor Pavarotti changed his mind about singing, thinking it inappropriate to perform in a banquet room. My arrangements were cancelled, but Steve Stavro, who was then a director of Maple Leaf Gardens, came to Villa Columbo's rescue. Steve and his wife, Sally, graciously offered their house for a black-tie affair. A hundred people were invited at a thousand dollars a person. I was again able to arrange donations of liquor and wine and we attended the event as the Stavros' guests.

Steve Stavro

After all the guests had mingled and enjoyed their cocktails, Senor Pavarotti arrived with his father, a fine singer in his own right, and was introduced to everyone. When it came to my introduction, he gave a look of some recognition, though he obviously couldn't quite decide where he had seen me before. I smiled and pointed to my bracelet. He said, "Ah, Luciano." He gave me a big hug and introduced me to his father. We had a wonderful evening. The great man was very kind and generous with his time, going to each of the ten tables (each named after an operatic masterpiece) and having a picture taken with the guests at each. It was an evening I will always treasure.

Gino Emprey

I last saw Gino backstage at Tony Bennett's concert at the Fallsview Casino in Niagara Falls in June of 2006. Nikki Pezaro telephoned me at the end of August telling me that Gino had a very bad stroke while visiting Ann and Ed Mervish and was in the hospital not able to communicate.

I was sad to hear the news even though Gino and I had many differences when he was entertaining director for the Imperial Room. I felt it was a very sad way for Gino to be in that state after working so hard and being a very successful publicist, agent and entertainment director.
There are many tales of Gino inside these pages as Paul Russell and Robert Jeffery were helping me craft this novel from the beginning of 1990. Gino passed away in October of 2006 and my daughter, Patti, and I went to the funeral where Gino had a great send off.

Rest in peace, Gino. ~ Louis~

Great Songstresses

Helen O'Connell

Helen O'Connell was a great singer way back when I was still in my teens. She made a big impression when she joined the Jimmy Dorsey band in 1939 and her recordings of "Green Eyes," "Tangerine," and other songs in the early forties were played on jukeboxes all the time. She was on television a lot in its early days, and I was surprised she was still on the road and performing when she came to the Imperial Room in 1980.

Whenever I'd go backstage to see her, she'd always be doing exercises of some sort. She was sixty at the time, and she told me the exercises were good for her breathing. I thought her show was very good, and audiences seemed to agree. But I still remember the responses of two critics who came to Helen's early show, then went up to the Hook and Ladder Club to catch Teresa Brewer's late show. One wrote a good review about Helen and a bad one for Teresa. The other wrote the reverse. Not everyone sees a show in the same light.

Kay Starr

I recall as a young kid standing in line at the Casino Theatre on Queen Street to see Kay Starr perform. She was more of a jazz singer in those days—she'd worked with Glenn Miller's band and Charlie Barnet's—but later, in the 1950's, she crossed over into the commercial pop field and became a huge success. Her recordings of "Hoop-Dee-Doo" and "Wheel of Fortune" became classics of the time. She also had hits with "Rock and Roll Waltz" and "My Heart Reminds Me."

In the sixties, she dropped off the pop charts, but surfaced again in Las Vegas. She had a pretty good career performing in night clubs. We had her twice, in 1970 and 1973, and she did very well both times. Kay had a very strong, but pleasant personality, and we developed a good relationship. In later years, whenever she was performing in the States and fans mentioned they had seen her at the Imperial Room, she always sent me a note.

In the 1990's, I saw her perform with a couple of other stars of that earlier era, Helen O'Connell and Margaret Whiting. Before the show, we had coffee and she said, "Come walk with me." We had a little stroll and reminisced about the glory days of the Royal York. Sadly, when it came to the performance, she wasn't in good voice and went on and on about how she had a cold. Mention it once, fine, but don't go on about it. It was a very difficult night for a great star who had given us so many great songs.

Rosemary Clooney

Rosemary Clooney was a wonderful singer who probably deserved to be talked about in the same league with people like Sarah Vaughn or even Ella Fitzgerald. But her commercial success with songs like "Come On-a My House," "This Ole House," and "Hey There" made people look at her in a different way. She was popular on television in the fifties and did a star turn with Bing Crosby and Danny Kaye in the movie, "White Christmas."

Unfortunately, her career—and her life—took a terrible downturn when she was near her good friend, Bobby Kennedy, when he was shot in Los Angeles. It took her years to recover from the trauma, but she came back strong. When we had her at the Imperial Room in the mid-seventies, she put on a very good show and was well received. She did very good business.

She was a lovely lady and very sociable. I spent a lot of time with her backstage. I think she needed a lot of company to help deal with her manic depression. When she came back a second time, she didn't do as well. She had become extremely heavy by then, but could still sing beautifully.
On one of her opening nights, as was the rule, all the staff had to leave the room so there wouldn't be any noise or service, as it interfered with the artist's performance. On this particular night one of my waiters went by me when the show had been on for five minutes, carrying four or five trays stacked precariously on top of each other, the topmost tray full of dirty dishes. The lights were out, the show was on and I realized that with the trays overlapping, there would be an accident. He went by a table near the rails, and not surprisingly, the top tray with its coffeepot and ketchup fell on Mr. and Mrs. McDonald's table below. The Curtis family was seated below the MacDonald table with their eight-year-old daughter (who is now a doctor). I see them once in a while and have a laugh about the whole incident.

I'll never forget how Rosemary Clooney looked down at the bedraggled couple and asked, "Are you all right, dear?" That's how sensitive she was. Needless to say, the waiter heard about it.

Another evening, as I was walking by the table of a Mr. and Mrs. Henderson close to the entertainment, Mr. Henderson picked up a piece of grilled salmon and was about to eat it when he suffered a massive coronary and died instantly. I pulled the chair away from the table, placed him behind the pillar, called 911, and the show went on.

We wanted Rosemary back again, but, as so often happened when a star's popularity diminishes, we knew she couldn't fill the room herself, so we booked her with Myron Cohen, another frequent guest who could no longer fill the place up on his own. Between the two of them, they did just fine.

Patti Page

Patti Page had some of the most memorable hit songs of the early 1950's. I remember singing along with songs like "With My Eyes Wide Open I'm Dreaming" and "Cross Over the Bridge," dancing to "The Tennessee Waltz" (didn't everybody?), and even enjoying the rather silly song, "(How Much Is) That Doggie in the Window."

Her career had slipped a bit by the time she came to the Imperial Room in 1973. I think she was going through some problems in her life at the time. But she never quit working (she won a Grammy Award in 1998!) and put on a good show. She sang well and was a very nice person, with a soft-spoken, southern charm.

Della Reese

Della Reese was a major star who started singing with Mahalia Jackson's gospel group way back in the 1940's and had a big hit with "And That Reminds Me" in 1957. She attracted quite a following after appearing on Ed Sullivan's Sunday night show 20 times and having her own syndicated TV show in the late sixties. Forty years later, she was still on television every week in "Touched By An Angel."

She put on a terrific show, though she sometimes got a little political in her patter. We got to be pretty good friends, and I often dined with her. She was very charming, a smart lady, and, obviously a very talented one.

Vikki Carr

We were excited about having Vikki Carr perform in 1977. Her career had taken off in the late sixties when she had a few hits, the biggest one being "It Must Be Him." She often appeared on television shows, especially with Dean Martin and Carol Burnett, so she had quite a following.

She was a great singer. Unfortunately, she also had a real problem with cigarette smoke. Given the habits of the time, working in nightclubs might not have been the best career move. I could sympathize with her. I could even accept that she asked the guests not to smoke while she was on. But I, along with many guests, thought it was too much that her act often consisted of her talking about the evils of smoking for more than a half hour, then singing for maybe twenty-five minutes. She seemed determined to convert the audience. I had to tell her, "I'm sorry you have a problem, but people pay a cover charge to see you entertain, not for a lecture." We never invited her back.

Natalie Cole

Natalie Cole had a lot of success in the late 1970's, mainly with R&B hits that she sang in a style very different from that of her late father, Nat 'King' Cole. When she came to the Imperial Room in 1983, she wasn't a major mainstream star and was at a low point in her life, both professionally and personally. She was a nice person, but it was certainly obvious to me that she had a lot of problems.

Later in her career, after she had matured, her voice mellowed and she had a huge hit singing a duet with her dad's version of "Unforgettable." When she was with us, however, her voice was very high and her style of singing wasn't conducive to the Imperial Room. It was very loud and not very melodic and our older audiences were not ready for it. The show wasn't all that great either, so our audience, such as it was, didn't show that much appreciation. I wish we could have had her ten years later.

Charo

When she came to Toronto in March 1974, Charo was known for marrying band leader Xavier Cugat in Caesar's Palace in Las Vegas when she was (supposedly) 15 years old and for appearing in several movies and on many TV shows. She was called the "Cuchi-Cuchi Girl" (her trademark phrase) and was sometimes mocked for flaunting her physical gifts on stage. She was extremely well endowed and dressed to display her assets to the best effect.

But, in fact, she was quite a good singer and dancer and a talented comedienne who didn't seem to get the kind of appreciation she really deserved. She was also an excellent musician. In later years, even a magazine for professional guitar players named her "Best Flamenco Guitarist."

Backstage, she was a shy and sweet person. During her run, she was invited to a lot of parties, but wouldn't go unless I came along. A friend of mine wanted to entertain Charo and her sister on a Sunday night, and she agreed – again, as long as I went with her. Years later, I saw her perform in a terrific show in Florida. I sent my card backstage and she rushed right out and said, "Why didn't you tell me you were coming? You'd have been my guest."

Connie Francis

I first met Connie Francis when I was Maitre D' of the Black Knight Room. She came in for dinner with her father, George, and both proved to be delightful people. By that time, Connie had built on her huge success with "Who's Sorry Now?" and with movie appearances and other hits like "Lipstick on Your Collar" and "Where the Boys Are." We had a good conversation and she left me a nice photo of herself seated chastely but suggestively on a chesterfield. Years later, when she appeared in the Imperial Room, I brought the picture in for her to sign. I guess she'd grown tired of the pose, since I never got the photo back.

We booked her in the short time she returned to performing between the years when she was recovering from a brutal beating and rape and another period of depression after her brother was gunned down. Between those times, she worked hard to revive her career, and she put on an extremely good show for us.

We had a wonderful week, though her manager was always after me to get more people in the room. Connie was working on a percentage basis, and there had to be so many people in the room for her to make good money. With some artists, Tony Bennett for example, guests brought their families and there would be tables of eight, ten, or twenty, so it was easy to accommodate 450 people. But with others, such as Connie, there were always lots of tables of two, making it difficult to get more than 375 people in the room. I had a terrible time, but I managed it, though some nights people had to pull in their stomachs to move between the tables, things being so tight.

Years later, Connie and I had a friendly reunion backstage at a Tony Bennett concert in Fort Lauderdale, Florida. It was unfortunate that a woman of such talent had to suffer so many hard times in her life, and it's good to see her still performing and doing so well in the 21st century.

Sarah Vaughn

I admired Sarah Vaughn tremendously from the first time I heard "Tenderly," her big hit from 1947. I loved all her songs and loved the way she sang, with a range that could take her higher up and lower down than almost any other singer. Even Ella Fitzgerald called her the world's "greatest singing talent," and I was very happy to welcome her to the Imperial Room.

Her adoring fans called her "Sassy" or "the incomparable Sarah," and usually attended her shows in great numbers. The first time, she appeared however, she arrived just in time for the show, whether because she came late to town or because she didn't think it necessary to have a sound check for the sound system as all artists did every day. The show went on and was a disaster. She was roundly criticized by the press, and sales slumped over her ten-day run, even though she made a point of checking the sound from the second day on. The damage had been done.

But she came back again a couple of years later and we had a wonderful two weeks with her. She checked the sound, the show went on the way it should, and the audiences showed up as we had hoped and expected.

Petula Clark

Petula Clark first made a name for herself in North America with the release of "Downtown" in 1965. She followed that up with a string of hits such as "I Know A Place," "My Love," "A Sign of the Times," "I Couldn't Live Without Your Love," "Color My World," and "Don't Sleep in the Subway." Not many on this side of the Atlantic knew that she began her career as a child performer during the war and continued it through the 1950's with appearances in many British films and with a good many British hit songs.

She was a superstar. I'd met her a couple of times during the sixties when she performed at the Canadian National Exhibition, and was certainly looking forward to having her appear in the Imperial Room. She was friendly right from the beginning, and would come down every afternoon to check the sound system and chat.

She put on a great show and audiences loved her. What impressed me most was the courage and professionalism she showed during an uncomfortable incident about the fourth night of her engagement. A middle–aged couple came to see the late show, and the lady informed me it was her husband's birthday. They were beautifully dressed for the occasion, obviously preparing for a memorable night out. Because it was such a special outing, I put them at a table quite close to the stage.

Everything was going along wonderfully until Petula started to sing "Don't Cry for Me, Argentina." I heard a terrible commotion close to the front and immediately rushed to where the sound was coming from. The birthday table was almost on its side and the food and settings were falling to the floor as the man stood up and yelled, "Boo, get her off the stage. Get her off." I called security, who hustled the man out the door. It was one of the few times we had to physically remove a guest. I followed security out and, between tears and rage, the man told me he had lost a comrade in the Falklands War, which was then still underway. He said, "She's English. She's not supposed to sing songs like that. England's at war with Argentina. I'm not going to listen to her celebrate Argentina." Great trooper that she was, Petula kept singing beautifully throughout the entire incident.

Connie Stevens

Connie Stevens was an interesting woman, as well as a talented and beautiful one. She was really more of an actress than a singer, although she had a couple of hits in the fifties and sixties. Movies didn't make her much of a star either, but playing Cricket Blake in the "Hawaiian Eye" TV series did.

She appeared at the Imperial Room twice -- once in 1977 and again in 1983. The five years between visits was more because of her busy schedule than any lack of a Toronto audience. She had developed her nightclub talents over many years in Las Vegas, so she put on a very polished show. She was smart and sharp (as her later success as a business tycoon showed) and was always cordial, on and offstage.

Wanda Cannon

Wanda Cannon was a beautiful young lady with a beautiful voice who often sang with the Howard Cable Orchestra. During her engagements, we spoke every day and I had dinner many nights with her and her husband, Bob, a wonderful guy and chiropractor to many of the dancers in Toronto. Connie Stevens' manager, after hearing Wanda sing, approached Howard to ask that he not allow Wanda to sing that week with his band. He (the manager) would pay for her missed week. Why did he do this? He recognized that Wanda had a very good voice and was trying to eliminate competition between her and Connie.

Wanda got a week's paid holiday. I personally felt that Connie did not know anything that had transpired between her manager and Howard Cable. There was no need for such a transaction because Connie had a wonderful voice, her own style and was a captivating entertainer. Everyone loved her. She did good business and we welcomed her back at other times. Wanda went on to do big things, appearing in many sitcoms and television dramas and landing quite a few good roles in American movies (she played Robert Duvall's wife in Arnold Schwarzenegger's "The 6th Day," for example), as well as Canadian ones. One was "For the Moment," a 1993 movie set in Manitoba.

It told the story of airmen from different Commonwealth countries who trained in western Canada before flying bombers into combat during World War II. Wanda was cast as a lady who took care of the airmen's sexual needs "for the moment." I saw it three or four times on the movie channel before I realized that one of the main characters was played by Russell Crowe who was just starting out in his North American film career. I phoned and told her how proud I was of her. As Wanda was very shy, I avoided mentioning the nude scene. I did mention that she must have gotten very friendly with Russell Crowe. She thought he was a wonderful guy and she was proud he went on to become such a super actor.

She and Bob moved to Vancouver to be closer to the film industry scene in the late 1990's, but each year she calls on my birthday to sing me her best wishes for the day. She's a wonderful person, and I'm so happy she has done so well.

Pearl Bailey

The first time Pearl Bailey came to the Imperial Room was in the spring of 1979. She'd been around an awful long time by then, but she hadn't played a nightclub in six years. I thought this was kind of odd for someone who had started singing in gin joints in Philadelphia when she was still a teenager, moved up to clubs like the Village Vanguard and Blue Angel in New York in the 1940's, and had played some of the biggest places in the world during the 1960's.

But she had created a new career for herself in the decade before she came to us, making a big splash as Dolly Gallagher Levi in an all-black production of "Hello, Dolly," both on Broadway, then on tour in Canada and the United States. Personally, I remembered her more from the movies like "Carmen Jones" and "Porgy and Bess" she had made in the 1950's. But she wanted to get back to the club world, and we were happy to book her.

Our relationship got off to a rocky start. At rehearsal, I noticed that our pull-out stage was out onto the small dance floor as far as it could go -- about twenty feet. Most nights, I only pulled it out about six feet so we could get tables right up to the stage and create a warm and good feeling of intimacy.

I always took the view that everyone should see the artist, not her backside. So I said to her, "Miss Bailey, with the stage so far out, what's going to happen is that you'll have all these people behind you."

She said, "You listen to me. I'm the boss. It's in my contract. I want the stage out. This is the way it's going to be."

"All right, Miss Bailey, whatever you say."

I always gave stars as much latitude as they wanted, but I wasn't happy with her attitude. She was curt, tough, and too bossy, so I pretty much avoided her. As it turned out, she had good reason for insisting on the extended stage. I hadn't seen her act, so I didn't know it involved a lot of walking around, entertaining everyone on the floor. I didn't really appreciate that she was known as much for her mischievous humor as her singing. Sometimes it seemed there was a little too much of the humor and not enough of the singing. On opening night, I discovered the biggest part of her act was reminiscing, adlibbing, making random observations about whatever crossed her mind, doing double-takes and dances, and generally clowning around. Then she'd sing a few songs, mainly standards. She still had one hell of a voice. She even brought me into the act. We had the same birthdays—she turned sixty-one the day I turned fifty-one on the day she opened—and we were featured in a newspaper photo sharing a huge cake. The audience that night spontaneously broke into "Happy Birthday." Then in the middle of her act, I heard, "Luigi, come up here." That didn't make me happy either. I didn't like Luigi. It's Luciano. "Let's sing a song together." With that, Pearl started singing "You Light Up My Life." Being a ham, I didn't mind singing a few lines with her, but only when she told me to. I even smiled only when she told me to.

Her whim seemed to be law. She ran the show just the way she wanted. Even during the first song, "Smile," she got a few notes into it, noticed some musical problem, stopped everything, griped, then reintroduced herself and started again. Between songs, she interacted with our guests quite a bit, though sometimes in the same aggressive way I'd seen earlier. She told them that when she had worked at the old Casino in Toronto, she'd received six standing ovations and she expected the same from them. She didn't say it in a humorous way.

She also complained a lot, as if the audience wasn't even there. The band was too loud, the lights were too dim, she needed a chair, she needed a hankie, she needed a glass of water. She had me running around all night, except for when she told me to leave her alone. She criticized select musicians, though she seemed to let her husband of forty years, one of the greatest drummers in the world and a fantastic band leader, Louis Bellson, off the hook.

That wasn't always the way it was offstage. The second time she came, in 1983, someone broke into her hotel room and stole her fur coat. We moved her to another suite. She thought she saw a suspicious character hovering around and came down to the lobby terrified. We soon had the police on the case, but she became very upset with Bellson since he didn't seem to be doing anything about it, berating him in front of many people. She kept being tough on him backstage that night. She wouldn't go on and perform. It was left to me to get up on stage, stall, apologize to a room full of people, and try to calm the audience down while she let go in her dressing room. One hour later she cancelled the show.

We had another set-to when she appeared for a third time in 1986. The deal with most artists was that they took a percentage of the cover charge as part of their fee. Pearl took it all. That was fine the first couple of times. She did good business, selling out most nights and all for a cover charge. The third time around though she was getting a little passé. How often do people want to see Pearl Bailey giving the same show, spending all that money for food, drinks, parking, and all the rest? Some nights for the second show, there was hardly anyone there at all.

Whenever that happened over the years, I'd usually ask people from the front office to come in. I'd seat them ringside to make the place look good and make the artist feel better. When Pearl looked at the receipts for the night, she thought she was getting gypped. I explained the situation and what I had done. She said, "I don't care if the place is empty. I want everyone sitting there to pay the cover charge. See to it." I stopped bringing people in and had to pay the cover charge for the staff.

For all our troubles, we did have better moments. We'd often talk in her dressing room. Once, she proudly showed off a very small television she had in the room. I marveled at its miniature size, which I'd never seen at the time.

She said, "I've got about eight or nine of them back home. I'll send you one."

She later sent me a collection of the six books she'd written about her life, her education, cooking, and various other experiences, along with a Louis Bellson album. A few weeks later, she sent a note, asking if I'd received them. I wrote back, saying, "Yes, I got your package. Thanks. But did the TV set possibly get lost?" She never wrote back.

Pearl had a strong religious and humanitarian side too. That went back to her roots. She'd never actually had any formal musical training. She learned to sing at age three at the Pentecostal church in Philadelphia where her father was the preacher. Her evangelical streak stayed with her. President Richard Nixon appointed her as America's "Ambassador of Love" and she served as a special goodwill ambassador to the United Nations for Presidents Ford, Reagan, and George Bush (the elder). She sent me a picture of her with Ronald Reagan after he sent her to spread good cheer in Egypt. She even went back to the university later in life and graduated from Georgetown University with a bachelor's degree in theology when she was sixty-seven years old.

She once said, "What the world really needs is more love and less paperwork." I got that message first hand. The third time she appeared in the Imperial Room, she learned about the controversy and disagreements Gino Empry and I were having at the time. She called us both into her dressing room to speak "the word of Jesus," that we should at least try to like each other more. Her gesture didn't help.

Pearl was a gifted artist. She remained an exceptional singer to the end of her years, but to me she was more a "personality," an absolute original, and that made her a great star.

Classic Voices

Billy Daniels

Billy Daniels was one of the finest entertainers I ever met. I was a big fan of his from his early days in radio and films, though I naturally never got to see his legendary nightclub performances, especially in New York, during the forties and fifties. He was a pioneer too, becoming the first black entertainer to host his own television show. He'd gone on to appear on Broadway with Sammy Davis Jr. in the sixties. After he appeared at the Imperial Room in 1973, he went on to perform with Pearl Bailey in the all-black production of "Hello, Dolly" in 1975.

Billy was very warm, always very nice, and a great showman. He was extraordinary and filled the room every night. When he went into his signature song, "That Old Black Magic," girls and women of a certain age would melt. They'd go crazy over him, which was always fun to watch.

Billy Eckstine

Like Billy Daniels, by the time Billy Eckstine came to us in 1973, he was a real heart throb to people thirty or forty years old. He wasn't just a singer, but a bandleader and musician who played several instruments and at one time or another had in his bands people who would go on to be some of the greatest names in jazz, like Charlie Parker, Dexter Gordon, Dizzy Gillespie, Miles Davis, Art Blakey, Lena Horne, and Sarah Vaughan. He was a big influence on the hipsters and jazz guys in the late forties and fifties, not only with his music but with the way he dressed and carried himself.

But the be-bop crowd didn't come to the Royal York. So it was mostly the old ballads he was famous for—"Blue Moon," "Caravan," "You Go to My Head"—that got the Imperial Room audience swooning. Swoon they did, and they came in droves to see this great entertainer.

Ed Ames

The Ames Brothers were one of the greatest male quartets of the 1950's. They had quite a few recording hits and appeared on Ed Sullivan's TV show numerous times. Ed Ames left the group to go out on his own, both as a singer and an actor in musicals and straight plays. Many people never realized that he starred in stage productions of "The Crucible" and "One Flew Over the Cuckoo's Nest."

He was a nice guy and a great singer who performed some of the old songs he did with his brothers, as well as the few solo hits he had, especially "Try to Remember" from the off-Broadway hit, "The Fantasticks," which he had starred in for some time. He was pretty good at humor too and naturally made reference to his famous moment on the Johnny Carson show in 1965 when he threw a tomahawk across the stage at a chalk outline of a cowboy and hit it in the groin. It's a moment still replayed endlessly on TV since it got the loudest and longest bout of laughter in the show's history, which was quite a feat.

Pat Boone

In the mid-seventies, the great Pat Boone was pretty much only recording gospel and religious records, many of them with his family. But he still had an act that built on his success and fame of the 1950's and 1960's when he was the most popular singer in America after Elvis Presley. He made quite a few movies, too, including Rodgers and Hammerstein's "State Fair," a personal favorite.

Pat was a gentleman and one of the most well-mannered people I ever met. He matched his white-bucked, clean-cut, God-fearing image perfectly. He was the real thing. Our audiences loved him as he sang all his old songs—"April Love," "Love Letters in the Sand," "Moody River," and so on. He gave a very good show.

Don Ho

Don Ho made a name for himself as a musician and singer in his native Hawaii in the early 1960's. When he released his debut album in 1965, he moved on to play some of the premier spots in Las Vegas, Lake Tahoe, and New York.

Most people in North America only became aware of him when he recorded an odd song called "Tiny Bubbles" that kept him on the pop charts for quite some time. He appeared on several television shows (even "The Brady Bunch") and had his own variety series, "The Don Ho Show," for a few months in the mid-seventies.

I liked his singing. A lot of other people in Toronto obviously did too. As soon as it was announced that we had booked him, reservations poured in like crazy. His shows sold out well in advance.

I greeted him warmly the afternoon he arrived, and he responded in kind. But I was a little concerned that he had six huge, burly, Hawaiian bodyguards with him. They dedicated themselves to keeping everyone away from Don, including me. Their attitudes and actions didn't make for a very comfortable atmosphere. But after a couple of nights, they saw that I was only trying to be helpful to him and they took me into their fold. When I was finally able to go into the dressing room and talk with him, I found Don to be a wonderful man.

Robert Goulet

I had known Robert Goulet when he was a Canadian television star on Sunday night's "Showtime" in the 1950's. He came to the Imperial Room often to dine. He also came with friends to celebrate his leaving for New York in 1960, when he made his name in America playing opposite Julie Andrews and Richard Burton in the original production of "Camelot."

He was always popular with Toronto audiences, so we had him a couple of times. He always sold out. I was happy to find out that his success on Broadway and in Hollywood and Las Vegas never changed him. He was fun backstage and always sociable to everyone, including the busboys and waiters, which wasn't all that normal for the bigger stars. He also came to see one of his former wives, Carol Lawrence, perform.

Carol Lawrence

When I went to Vegas, he came to my table and we chatted for a while. For a few years he and his wife sent me Christmas cards.

John Gary

To my mind, if anyone should have achieved superstardom but didn't, it was John Gary. He had one of the most beautiful voices imaginable.

He had a great vocal range and sang the great song standards, mainly romantic ballads and love songs, in his own unique style. I loved his clarity and the sincerity and feeling he put into the songs. One critic summed him up as "poised, polished, and perfect." That was about right.

It's not that he didn't achieve a great deal of success. He replaced Sonny and Cher on TV in the summer and made a tremendous number of albums that sold pretty well. But he kind of stayed just under the radar of really popular acclaim. Our audiences liked him so much, however, that we had him back many times. People loved him. He filled up the room at the beginning, though it wasn't as full at the end of his string of appearances.

He was an engaging and very interesting man, not only a singer but a former marine, an inventor, sculptor, poet, songwriter, archer, tennis player, and writer. He even held underwater endurance records and patented a couple of deep-sea propulsion devices. He could talk about anything. He was a generous man too. One time I was in Florida when he was playing at the Galt Ocean Mile, quite a big place that was hard to get into without reservations far in advance. I phoned him to see if I could get tickets. I ended up taking eight people with me and John picked up the whole tab.

Mel Torme

Mel Torme was one of the few male artists in the same league as Frank Sinatra and Tony Bennett. He had a much higher voice than those two, though he had a good vocal range and always sang in the smooth style that got him the nickname "Velvet Fog." I always liked his stuff, from the forties right through to the eighties.

He appeared twice at the Imperial Room, once alone and once with the great blind pianist, George Shearing, a big star in his own right, and Don Thompson, the terrific bass player from Toronto. They were fabulous together. Mel himself wasn't overly nice on a personal level. He could be a bit abrupt. But he sold out the room. For more than sixty years in the business, Mel was never short of admirers.

Buddy Greco

Buddy Greco was never a superstar, but he was a fine entertainer, a pianist and singer who'd played in Benny Goodman's band. He had a few hits like "The Lady Is A Tramp" and recorded an awful lot of albums and singles. He made it big in Vegas too, sometimes performing with the Rat Pack at the height of their notoriety. He often played in Toronto at the Town Tavern, the local spot for most jazz artists, but he had a broader audience than that, so we brought him in a couple of times.

His last performance at the Imperial Room was for our usual big New Year's Eve event in 1985. Gino had also booked a comedy act to go on before Buddy. When I first met these four young men, I was having my lunch on New Year's Eve. They asked if I was Gino Empry, but I apologized, saying I didn't know where he was.

When it came to midnight, the balloons came down, people danced for about fifteen minutes, the champagne corks popped, and everybody was happy. Then Howard Cable's band left the stage for a break and the comedy troupe came out. I went off to relax and have some champagne myself. It wasn't too long before I heard, "Boooo! Get the hook. Boooo." A guest, one of our regulars, found me and said, "What's going on? This is a terrible act. You've got to do something."

By the time I could observe the scene, the situation was obviously deteriorating badly. I went backstage to demand Gino do something, to get them off and get Buddy Greco out there early. He got down on his knees and said, "What do you want from me? You want to crucify me? I'm not Jesus Christ."

I went back out front and everything was going crazy. Guests were throwing things at the stage and booing with great gusto. The performers were telling the guests to go f… themselves. I went up on stage and tried to take the mic from one of the performer's hands. It got to be a tug of war as he said, "What are you doing?"

"Let me have the mic, please." He finally handed it to me and the whole troupe moved to the side of the stage. I stood there in my tuxedo, the spotlight on me, and looked out over 400 people, most in tuxes and gowns, and all very, very disturbed.

I didn't want to chastise the artists. It wasn't their fault. So I simply said, "Happy new year. Ladies and gentlemen, as you know, the Royal York Hotel has always tried to bring the best of entertainment to the Imperial Room. Unfortunately, these very talented young artists are here at the wrong place and at the wrong time. I'm sure that, in the very near future, you'll recognize these artists for their talents, maybe on your television screens. But we have made a tremendous mistake. A big mistake. Please forgive us. We do, however, have Buddy Greco, a very fine artist, who'll come out to entertain you shortly, and I hope you enjoy the show. Again, happy new year."

The people gave me a nice round of applause and the room settled down. I went over to the door and started crying like a baby. David Oliver, who was managing the Royal York at the time, came over and put his arm around me. I said, "How could you let that son-of-a-bitch destroy this room?"

The parents of the young men, who were in the audience, thanked me on the way out. Those young men, called "The Kids in the Hall," later became famous with their own television show.

Best of Broadway

Bernadette Peters

Of all the Broadway divas who appeared at the Imperial Room, Bernadette Peters was my all-time favorite, and not just because she was Italian (she was born Bernadette Lazarra, but changed her name to avoid typecasting).

What a talent. She'd been working in show business since she was three years old and her experience showed. She was the embodiment of professionalism. She'd been in many Broadway shows and, while she hadn't yet won her two Tony Awards for Best Lead Actress in a Musical, she had been nominated several times. She also made an impression in the Steve Martin movie, "The Jerk."

She didn't draw as well as she should have. Not enough people were aware of her yet. But she put on a great show. She was a lovely lady with a terrific voice and was as warm in person as she was onstage. I'd bring her on and off stage and, when we came off, she'd always give me a little squeeze. What a pleasure she was to work with. I thought she was a genius.

Chita Rivera

Chita Rivera was a great performer on stage. By the time she came to us, she was actually getting on in years for someone who was primarily a dancer, trained as a ballerina as a child. She had first become a star in 1957 when "West Side Story" opened. She got even bigger with "Bye Bye, Birdie" in 1960. But she never let age get her down. She worked her heart out, which is how she could manage to still perform in demanding musical theater roles into the 1990's.

She was a beautiful person, a wonderful lady who was perhaps the least egotistical performer I ever met. With her honest, direct manner and obvious dedication to doing what she loved, she charmed and entertained audiences as much as she charmed me.

Melba Moore

Melba Moore made a name for herself on Broadway in the original production of "Hair," replacing (of all people) Diane Keaton. She won a Tony Award, for the musical, "Purlie." when she was twenty-five years old. With that under her belt, she got a recording contract and attracted a sizable following.

On the strength of that, we booked her for a run in the Imperial Room. It was a mistake. On Broadway, there are a lot of supporting people around. On a nightclub stage, there's no one else and she was alone under the spotlight in front of hundreds. Her voice was very high, operatic even, and that kind of voice is not really suited to a nightclub.

The crowds stayed away. It didn't help that Blake Kirby's horrendous review in The Globe and Mail was headlined "Melba Moore Disaster in the Imperial Room."

Anthony Newly

Anthony Newly was one name that often came up during the meetings of our talent committee. Zena Cheevers kept recommending him and, every time, I'd ask, "After one song—'What Kind of Fool Am I?'—what's he got? What's he going to do? On Broadway you have a supporting cast behind you, but it's a different story when you're up there alone trying to entertain for an hour."

Fortunately, for all the time Gordon Cardy was general manager he accepted my thoughts. When I lost control of booking the room, Gino Empry brought up Newly too, and I said the same thing. Gino booked him anyway, against my advice and for a substantial amount of money.

He was a nice enough fellow, but he didn't have much of an act. He simply wasn't that entertaining, and the word got around quickly enough. The crowds did not come out. We lost a lot of money that week.

Peter Allen

Peter Allen had a fine career as a cabaret performer and eventually as a songwriter and Broadway star. He was an Australian who had been discovered by Judy Garland and was married to her daughter, Liza Minnelli, for a few years in the late sixties. He really made his mark in the mid- to late-seventies. He recorded albums, played the New York nightclub circuit, wrote songs like "Don't Cry Out Loud" for Melissa Manchester and "I Honestly Love You" for Olivia Newton John, and even won an Academy Award for co-writing the theme for the Dudley Moore movie, "Arthur."

He was a terrific singer and a fantastic musician, playing piano in a very flamboyant, almost outrageous way. What a showman! I also found him to be a very fine gentleman, always courteous and very nice. We had a wonderful week with him, with his shows sold out every night. He enjoyed being at the Imperial Room, and was always complimentary about the audiences and the way I ran the room.

At the end of his run, he gave me a big hug and slipped something into my jacket pocket. I said, "Thank you so much, Peter, and I hope we see you again. You were great. The best of luck to you." Needless to say, as I left the room, I reached into my pocket. I took out one Canadian dollar. I was sure he meant to give me a much different kind of bill, especially since the Canadian dollar at the time looked much like an American hundred. I didn't know whether to go back and say something to him or just forget about it. But then, I thought he might be upset when he found the hundred he meant to give me still in his own pocket. So I thought, 'What the heck.'

I went back to the dressing room and called him aside. "Peter, it's a bit embarrassing for me to say anything, but I know you meant well and would probably be upset if you found out later that this is what you gave me."

When I held out the dollar bill, he looked quite taken aback. He said, "Oh, Louis, I'm so sorry." He reached into his pocket and took out an American hundred. "This is what I meant to give you. And thank you for bringing it to my attention. Don't be embarrassed. I really appreciate it."

We parted as good friends and unfortunately, I never saw him again. It was a sad day when "The Boy from Oz" died so young from AIDS in 1992.

Joel Grey

Joel Grey was a phenomenal entertainer, a great actor and a very nice fellow who became one of the very few people who won both a Tony Award and an Academy Award for the same role (as the Master of Ceremonies in "Cabaret").

We had many conversations when he appeared at the Imperial Room. He told me that his father, Mickey Katz, had some close connection with Toronto, though he was born in Cleveland. Katz was a great Borscht Belt comedian and musician who performed with the crazy Spike Jones band. The family talent kept coming when Joel's daughter, Jennifer, made a big splash in "Dirty Dancing" and other movies.

Joel was such a success with Toronto audiences that we presented him four times, first in 1976 and finally in 1984. He had a wonderful way with people, on stage and off, and I always thought his many talents were best showcased in an intimate nightclub setting. Theatre-goers and movie-viewers would never be able to appreciate his full range and the star power he radiated so effortlessly.

Groups

The Fifth Dimension

The Fifth Dimension broke onto the music scene in a very big way in the 1960's. The five original members brought a lot of musical traditions to their work -- gospel, jazz, pop, opera, and rhythm and blues. They turned the combination into something that was really fresh. They had a string of very big hits like "Up, Up and Away," "Stoned Soul Picnic," "Aquarius/Let The Sunshine In," and "Wedding Bell Blues."

They were really big, winning Grammy Awards and appeared on every television show on the air at the time, from "The Ed Sullivan Show" and "Hollywood Palace" to specials with Frank Sinatra and even Woody Allen.

When they appeared at the Imperial Room in 1976, their career wasn't as hot, but they still showed a great combination of talent, energy, and warmth on stage and their harmonies were as interesting as ever. They were a pleasure to work with and drew good crowds.

Two of the original members, Marilyn McCoo and Billy Davis, a husband and wife team, weren't with the group at the time, having left to pursue a separate career. A couple of years later, we booked them by themselves. They put on a very nice show, very smooth, though nothing extraordinary.

Smothers Brothers

We booked the Smothers Brothers musical-comedy team in 1976. They'd been around for a long time by then, going back to late fifties and really hitting it big with their" Smothers Brothers Comedy Hour" on TV in the late sixties. That became a controversial show, which gave them a very high profile. They tried another series, "The Smothers Brothers Show," in 1975.

They performed their usual routines, singing and playing folk songs (with Dick on bass and Tommy on guitar) and getting into arguments about all sorts of silly things, often ending up with an apparently dim-witted Tommy saying his signature line: "Mom always liked you best."

They were nice guys. Off-stage, their roles were reversed from what they showed to the audience. Tom was the sharp one, running their business affairs. They were funny and did well, though not spectacularly so.

Sandler and Young

Tony Sandler and Ralph Young had an interesting act that was a little out of the ordinary. They were an odd couple -- Tony a Belgian well known in Europe for his singing, Ralph an American who was a very good singer and also did comedy with a Jewish touch. They had first made an impact in Las Vegas during the early sixties, then became regulars on all sorts of American TV shows, including Johnny Carson's and Ed Sullivan's (in fact, they performed on the very last "Ed Sullivan Show").

They sang great songs and harmonized beautifully. They had a unique style and sold millions of records. We had them at the Imperial Room three times in the early seventies. They were very nice and accommodating and did good business each time they came. When the act broke up, Tony came back in 1979 as a solo performer supported by the McCall Sisters. It wasn't the same. People came to see Sandler and Young as much for the comedy as the singing. On his own, Tony, as good as he was, didn't attract much of an audience.

Sergio Mendes Brasil Seventy-Six

Sergio Mendes had made a name for himself in the 1960's when bossa nova music seemed to take the world by storm. Sergio was a good piano player who did a good job of merging jazz and Latin American music. His Brasil 66 group had a couple of pretty big hits—"Mais Que Nada," "Fool on the Hill," "The Look of Love"—but after touring around with Herb Alpert and the Tijuana Brass for a few years, he kind of disappeared.

The group he brought to the Imperial Room in 1975 was almost a comeback attempt. It was a good band, with a couple of girl singers who did nice harmonies while the rhythm section barreled along. They didn't do bad business, mainly attracting people who remembered their earlier hits.

Irish Rovers

In the late 1970's, we booked the Irish Rovers to appear at the Imperial Room a couple of times. At that point, they were still known internationally mainly for "The Unicorn," their million-selling single from about ten years before. But in Toronto, they were even better known and liked for the television series they did for the CBC and Global television networks. They were good-time shows that were very popular. Being considered local talent, we could get them for about $1,500 a week.

I got to know the boys quite well, joining them in their dressing room to sing Irish songs. They were surprised I knew so many, but that was one of the benefits of attending St. Francis School. I spent quite a bit of time with the heavy-set fellow in the group, Jimmy Ferguson, who knew some of the players in my hockey league and often came to the games at George Bell Arena.

They put on great stage shows -- charming, rollicking, and rousing. Audiences loved them, feeling as if they were at a party among friends. It was a feeling they capitalized on with a big hit in the early eighties, "Wasn't That a Party." After that, we would have been lucky to get them for $50,000 a week.

I was honored that they invited me to their twenty-fifth anniversary celebration in Vancouver in 1989. I booked a flight and a suite, but at the last minute, couldn't go. Friends who were there told me the boys, not knowing I had to cancel, warmly introduced me from the stage.

In the 1990's, when I had my own restaurant, a couple of the Rovers came in to see me and share a few stories. They were great guys, and I was very saddened when Jimmy Ferguson passed away in 1997.

Blood, Sweat & Tears

Blood, Sweat & Tears was one of the most prominent jazz-rock groups of the late 1960's, though they didn't last long. Their reputation was really built on three songs: "You Made Me So Very Happy," "Spinning Wheel," and "And When I Die," all off the same 1969 album. But those songs were played constantly on radio for decades, so the name always had some cache.

The band sort of disappeared when the lead singer, David Clayton-Thomas, left for a solo career but got a new lease on life when he came back. He kept the band going for years. Clayton-Thomas was a local Toronto boy with whom I had had an unfortunate run-in in the early 1980's. He came to a late show at the Imperial Room wearing a leather bomber jacket, quite fashionable and acceptable apparel in later years, but not then, at least according to me. I thought he should be wearing a regular jacket and made an issue of it. He got upset with me, and eventually I let him in anyway.

When we booked the band later, David remembered the incident and reminded me of it. I said, "That was then, this is now. I'll do my best to see everything goes along smoothly." Everything did go smoothly and the band did quite well, attracting a good crowd.

The Pointer Sisters

The Pointer Sisters vocal group had a great deal of success during the 1970's and 1980's. When they started out, they sang forties-type songs, but eventually worked in a lot of different styles, from jazz and disco to country and western and soul. All four of the girls—Ruth, Anita, Bonnie, and June—were really good singers and very nice people.

The first time we had them, in 1977, they were still a quartet. The second time, in 1981, they had been a trio for some years after Bonnie left for a solo career. During those years, they had had their biggest success, with several very successful albums and more than a half dozen "top ten" singles, especially "Slow Hand" and "I'm So Excited."

They were a little different for the Imperial Room. They really rocked the place and always sold out. I remember one night when my back was just killing me. I said, "You know, you girls make me work too hard, getting 400 people in and out every night." The cause of my pain turned out to be kidney stones.

Some years later, I saw them perform in Las Vegas. They saw me in the front row, made quite a fuss, came down to shake my hand, and even asked me come up on stage with them. I declined, but I appreciated the gesture. I loved those girls.

In 1990, my daughter Patti was touring Europe. She was performing in Midem, Cannes at the Carlton. The Pointer Sisters were in the front row and couldn't believe that the kid they'd met years before in the Imperial Room was now in front of them. They couldn't wait to say hi and had Patti send a video message home to say hi to me and to say how happy they were for Patti.

Patti Jannetta

Of all my Imperial Room memories, the one I treasure most came in February of 1976. We had booked singer Julie Budd for a week. Budd was really just starting her career then, but had been attracting a lot of attention with her Barbra Streisand-like looks and manner as well as her terrific voice. She was a belter with a great vocal range.

Late in the day before she was to open, her manager called to say she was sick and couldn't make the engagement. There was no time to book anyone else out of New York. The hotel management thought we might have to close the room or go back to a simple dinner-and-dancing format. But I told Mr. Cardy that I knew a local band that played in clubs around town that was pretty good and was taking the week off for rest and rehearsal. I knew the band, Mixed Reaction, was available because the singer fronting it was my beautiful daughter, Patti, the oldest of my four children. Mr. Cardy was a little dubious at first, but I said, "Don't worry. They're good. They won't embarrass us." He said, "Whatever you say." Dave Baker, one of the four men, was Patti's husband.

Louis and Patti Jannetta

I called Patti right away and booked her. She and the four guys in the band were thrilled, in shock, and terrified all at the same time. Patti, of course, had been coming to the room since she was a child. She'd seen and met many of her musical idols on our stage. Part of her never thought she'd perform where they did. Part of her always dreamed of doing just that, though not on a twenty-four-hour notice.

Our publicist, Gino Empry, warned me that the critics who had planned to see Julie Budd were still coming. He specifically mentioned that the reviewer for The Globe and Mail, Blake Kirby, who wrote terrible reviews, had told Gino he'd definitely express his thoughts in print. I said, "Let him. He can't do any worse to Patti than he did to Melba Moore."

Caught off guard, the band admitted they weren't really ready for the room. But I told them, "Don't think about it. Just do it." Mixed Reaction was kind of a soft rock and disco quintet that put aside the disco for a few nights and did more R&B-oriented standards. They had no time to prepare arrangements, but they gave Howard Cable's band a list of songs and the keys they were in. Howard's musicians were so good they could play along with anyone, even without music on the stands.

Patti said she was "petrified" and that her "feet weren't even on the ground," but the opening show went from good to better and even better still. Some of the toughest critics in the city were there that night, and she got great reviews from all of them the next day. One praised her "self-possession and controlled energy." Even Blake wrote quite a good review, talking about her "strong, stylish voice" and her "youthful and likable personality." She performed between two great super stars, Marlene Dietrich and Ginger Rogers, who had a tough act to follow.

The band did good business the rest of the run, and, on the final night, got a standing ovation. We had lots of those in the Imperial Room, but this one was special. I joined in, of course, off to the side, hoping people wouldn't notice the tears in my eyes. I've never been prouder.

I never wanted Patti or any of my kids to go into show business. I'd seen too much heartache among the stars and didn't want any child of mine to have to go through some of the things I'd seen. But when she was in high school, just out of curiosity, Patti went to a local audition for a touring concert version of "Jesus Christ Superstar" and, for a lark, she sang. Victor Garber was one of her co-stars. She was hired on the spot. I wanted her to continue her education, but I came to accept her choice of a career. The standing ovation that night moved me a long way beyond acceptance.

The Imperial Room performance did good things for Mixed Reaction. Their fees went up and they got some guest shots on TV, better bookings around Toronto, and a tour of eastern Ontario.

Best of all, Doug Basset and Ted Delaney, two of the biggest executives at the Canadian Television Network (CTV), had seen the show and called to say they wanted her to do a Christmas special. It became "A Family Christmas with Patti Jannetta" with guests such as Barbara Hamilton, John Allen Cameron, and John McDermott, along with Corinne and me, husband, David, and daughters, Michelle and Ashley. It was a charming show and we loved doing it. Patti and I were featured on the cover of "Star Week" magazine, with the line, "Show business runs in the family," and an article inside calling us "the latest father-and-daughter combination in Toronto show business circles," a description I got a big kick out of. The special was shown annually for many years.

Jannetta Family Christmas

Bo Diddley, Louis & Patti Jannetta

It was another proud moment when Patti returned to the Imperial Room in 1988, this time in the company of Ronnie Hawkins and Bo Diddley. During the years between engagements, she'd performed across Canada, often opening for Hawkins. She'd married her first boyfriend and bass player in Mixed Reaction and had two beautiful daughters. She had recorded an album with a best-selling single. And, earlier in 1984, she'd been Canada's representative at Poland's huge musical Festival Sopot where she had performed for 50,000 and had been wined and dined and treated like a movie star and mobbed by 15,000 Poles. She even had her own bodyguards and photographers and appeared on the covers of European fashion magazines. The great Charles Aznavour presented her with the "Musicians' Favorite Award." She was later nominated for a Juno Award. By the time she came back to the Royal York, she'd more than paid her dues.

Ronnie Hawkins

We'd already had "Rompin' Ronnie" Hawkins perform in 1981 and again in 1982. I never thought he was the right kind of performer for a classy place like the Imperial Room. His show was always a little too raunchy and much too rockabilly for my taste. I always thought his was the kind of act that drove our regulars away. Later on though, Ronnie and I became very good friends.

In 1984, he tried harder to fit in with the character of the place. By that, I mean he wore a tux and tidied up his shaggy grey beard and hairdo. But he still told stories that I thought crossed the line. He invited women in the audience, some in their evening gowns, "to come up on the dance floor and shake your moneymakers." He rambled around the audience, trading quips with his friends while ignoring everyone else. He said things like, "The more you drink, the better I look. You might have to drink doubles, girls, but it's worth it in the end."

I wasn't too impressed, and some people in the audience seemed a little shell-shocked. But I have to admit he had people charged up when he and his band went through his own hits, some Elvis songs and a Chuck Berry medley, even if he forgot a few words here and there and had trouble hitting high notes. Then he introduced Patti, who really got the people going. She was polished and powerful.

Then Bo Diddley, dressed in flashy, blue chiffon, did a set, wailing away in his unique style. Bo was a good musician, but not a big personality in my view. He did have a lot of energy though, especially for someone who was 55 at the time, probably from loading up on carbohydrates; I had Bo up to my place in the country and he ate five plates of spaghetti. The best part of his set was a duet with Patti on "Make Up Your Mind Tonight," a tune they co-wrote and recorded together (she's the only female soloist to ever record a duet with Bo). Naturally enough, the show climaxed with six singers, four guitarists, and the rest of the band doing a boisterous version of "Hey, Bo Diddley."

To me, as well as many others, Patti was the best thing in the show. The reviewers said she was "a belter worth waiting for" and a "vivacious, talented singer with an impressive set of pipes," though one thought she was so classy she looked "out of place in the crowd of carousers."

But she showed she wasn't out of place and could even be a headliner when Ronnie Hawkins' heart problems took him off stage for the rest of the run and Patti carried on, fronting the show. It's not just a father talking when I say she belonged at the Imperial Room.

Comics

We always walked a fine line when it came to booking comedians in the Imperial Room. People's tastes in comedy vary so much, so comedians were an iffy proposition. Sometimes they did well, sometimes they really bombed. We could never be sure whether Toronto audiences would go for the Borscht Belt or Vegas styles still popular in the sixties and seventies or would gamble on something new. We pretty much stuck to people who were well known from television appearances, rather than some who were best known on the nightclub circuit.

Shecky Greene, for example, was one of the biggest stars in Las Vegas at one time, right up there with Johnny Carson, Bill Cosby, Buddy Hackett, and Don Rickles in his ability to headline shows at Vegas hotels. He was a great performer and, when his stock fell in Vegas, he'd often call me to ask if he could be booked. He would have done all right, but he wasn't all that well known to the broader audience and he always wanted too much money. Others had lots of TV exposure, and we usually did well with them.

Jackie Mason

I remember when Jackie Mason first hit the comedy scene in a big way around 1960. He had a sharp tongue and kind of a wicked attitude, which many people thought odd considering he was a rabbi. But he sure made people laugh with his jokes, his funny sideways looks, and his constant hand gestures. One not-very-nice gesture though got him into trouble when he made it at Ed Sullivan on live TV.

When we had him at the Imperial Room about 15 years later, his career was still suffering because of the fallout from that one little finger motion. It was too bad the shadow of it hung over him so long. He was quite brilliant in his way. He showed how brilliant with his one-man show on Broadway and other projects some years later. I thought he was great, and he did good business for us.

But he couldn't resist doing the one thing guaranteed to drive me up the wall. One night he said to people at a table down in front, "Hey, you must know Louis." Then he put out his palm and rubbed his fingers together. When he got off backstage, I said, "Don't you dare do that again. I don't need that. People are good to me, but I don't have my hand out. I'd appreciate it if you wouldn't do that." Thankfully, he stopped.

Jack Carter

Jack Carter was one of the few we did good business with. I thought he was pretty funny, though not as good as my favorite, Myron Cohen. But audiences liked him.

Jack and I had a good relationship, always friendly and easy-going. He even worked me into his act. He always praised the Imperial Room, saying how elegant it was with its beautiful chandeliers, how glorious and majestic. "Then you look at the door and there's that big Italian guy with no neck." I went to see him in Vegas and he repeated what he had said at the Royal York.

Myron Cohen

Myron Cohen had a special place in the world of comedy. He didn't tell jokes. He told stories, always speaking very slowly. I once heard someone refer to him as "an old Jewish Bill Cosby." His was an unhurried, deliberate style that was very different from the other Borscht Belt comics. He became more of a general star with his appearances on "The Ed Sullivan Show." Sometimes it seemed like he was on the show every week, but, in fact, it was only 47 times.

We had him at the Imperial Room five times in the 1970's. People loved his act. I did too. He never used a bad word, but he had me in stitches every time. The first time he was there, even Myron did the Maitre D' routine. The last night of his run, some local friends of his, Ben and Harry Smith, who owned the Prince George Hotel, were sitting right up front. He said, "Hey, Ben and Harry. You must know Louis." Then he made the typical hand gesture.

I knew he wasn't doing it just for laughs like Jackie Mason did, but I still had to say something when he got backstage. I said, "Myron, I know you meant well, but I don't appreciate that stuff."

Always the gentleman, he said, "I thought I was doing you some good. I'm sorry, Louis. Don't worry. I won't do it again." He was true to his word.

The last time he came, in 1983, he shared the bill with Rosemary Clooney. He always stood up while he did his act, but when he arrived in Toronto he tripped when he got off the plane and had to have a stool. He was in a lot of pain, but he carried on. He was even kind enough to come upstairs in the hotel, where a friend of mine was having a stag, to say a few complimentary things and tell a few stories. He was a generous man and I was proud to call him a friend.

Jackie Vernon

Jackie Vernon was a frequent and popular guest with Ed Sullivan and on other TV variety shows in the sixties and seventies. He was a lovely and very funny man with a low-key, dead-pan style that reminded me of Myron Cohen, but more self-deprecating. Most of his act was built around how, to look at him, it was hard to believe he was once considered a "dull guy," but his life had become much more exciting. Then he'd pretend to be showing slides of his latest vacation trip. ("Here I am tossing coins at the toll booth." (click) "Here I am under the car, looking for the coins.") He usually carried a broken trumpet around with him as a prop. He started his career as a trumpeter, so he could really play it, though he almost never did.

I liked his routines, but when he appeared at the Imperial Room, he hardly got any response at all. I tried to get things going by starting the applause as I did for so many artists, but not with all that much enthusiasm. About three days into his run, he told me he was Italian (he was born Ralph Veroni), so I started encouraging the audience with much more vigor.

He finished his run on a Saturday and was supposed to appear on "The Ed Sullivan Show" on Sunday, but fog had grounded all the planes leaving Toronto. Jackie offered me $750 if I would drive him to New York. I said sure, but the fog lifted, so I missed the chance to spend a great deal of time with him on the drive down. Jackie died young, but achieved a kind of immortality as the voice of Frosty in the "Frosty the Snowman" television show that became such a classic. It's still shown regularly almost forty years after its debut in 1969.

Jim Carrey

There were very few new or unknown talents booked into the Imperial Room over the years. The premier nightclub in the country was not the kind of place to hone an artist's talents or to ask guests to pay hefty prices for someone they didn't know. But there were a few little-known people who had the opportunity to perform there and who didn't disappoint.

When Gino Empry first booked a young Canadian boy from Newmarket -- Jim Carrey -- I had never heard of him at all. I was dubious about what he might do. By then, I had seen many great comedians, so I waited on opening night with some concerns. Jim came on stage, told a few jokes, and fell backwards in a way that made me surprised he didn't break his back. Then he went into his impressions, which I thought outdid even the great Rich Little, especially when he impersonated Henry Fonda in "On Golden Pond." He was hilarious and the Toronto audiences took to him in a big way.

He was also a very nice young man who would come by in the afternoons to say hello. I'd order him a sandwich and we'd sit and talk about anything and everything -- the city, or especially hockey. I was so happy that he went on to such incredible success as an actor, and proud to know that we at the Imperial Room may have played a small part in his achievement.

Phyllis Diller

Only Tony Bennett appeared more often in the Imperial Room than Phyllis Diller. She was such a funny lady. Except for the laughter, no one would hear a pin drop while she was onstage. Audiences loved her. I loved her too, and not only because she was so classy and did such great business. Whenever she did interviews on local TV or radio or with newspapers and magazines in Toronto, she always went out of her way to say that she only kept coming back because I ran the room so well and to say how much she appreciated the way I kept everything in order and first class.

We enjoyed many good times together, though she would seldom come down in the afternoons. We exchanged lots of showbiz stories about people and odd events we'd experienced. I told her that I had witnessed three deaths in the Imperial Room, two from guests choking on food caught in their throats, one from a massive heart attack. The heart attack victim, a regular seated near the stage at a table on the upper level behind the rail, was just putting a forkful of salmon to his mouth when the attack hit him. Rosemary Clooney was performing at the time. When I saw him slump over, I went to his aid, but knew immediately that he was dead. I moved him and his chair behind a column and went to call for medical help. The show went on as if nothing had happened. When I told Phyllis about it, she embellished the chair-moving story to outrageous proportions and worked it into her act, where it always received lots of laughs.

She was a great trouper. The only problem that ever came up was when she received her room bill on the last night during one engagement. A charge of $900 had been included. She called me, very upset, and said, "Louis, what's this? How did this get on my account?" It didn't take long to figure out that our publicist, Gino Empry, had entertained about ten of his friends one night and had signed her name to the tab by mistake. Needless to say, we took the charge off and dealt with Gino. The bill went on the entertainment account.

Craig Russell

Far worse, from many other points of view, was Craig Russell, who first appeared in 1979. He was probably one of the best-known female impersonators of the 1970's and 1980's. He'd become really famous after starring in a 1977 Canadian feature film, "Outrageous!" He usually played gay clubs and drag queen venues in Toronto and, after his movie success, across North America. But what he was doing in the Imperial Room, I could never understand.

I admit he was a genius in his way and he had a following. He was a good actor. He impersonated an awful lot of characters and did so very well -- Carol Channing, Marlene Dietrich, Judy Garland, Peggy Lee, Mae West, Janis Joplin, Bette Davis. What was really remarkable was his vocal range. High or low, he could do them all. He could even perform a duet between Ella Fitzgerald and Louis Armstrong and sound pretty good doing it.

While I admired his talent, I was appalled at some of his antics. He just wasn't right for our room. When he was doing Judy Garland, he wore tights and short shorts. I was told by some guests that his testicles were hanging out. And for the first time in the Imperial Room, I heard a four-letter word I wasn't happy to hear. As he was walking off the stage after one of his early shows, people stood and cheered and applauded very enthusiastically.

He said, "You want more?"

They all called out, "Yes. More. We want more."

"You want more?"

"Yeah."

He shot them a contemptuous look and said, "F… you," and walked off.

I went backstage, livid. "How dare you! How dare you treat our guests that way!" He couldn't respond in any way except by starting to cry. It was the beginning of a tough week. We never knew what to expect. Every time he did his act after that night, he'd look over to my desk after almost every number, give a mock bow, and say, "Is that all right, Mr. Jannetta?"

To me, he clearly had psychological problems, maybe from coping with too much success. He seemed to be in a never-ending battle with alcohol and drugs. I heard he was planning something spectacular for the last night of the run, going nuts in some way or other. I didn't know what he had in mind, but by then I was beyond embarrassment and reconciled to his idiosyncrasies.

That last night I had taken a reservation for a table of eight right up front. At the last minute, only four people showed up. As he came on stage to do his act, Craig looked at the four empty chairs and started yelling, "What's the matter, Mr. Maitre D', didn't they give you fifty dollars for the table?" I just stood at my desk, fuming. Then he started throwing the chairs around the room (after that, I never left empty chairs near the stage). Needless to say, I didn't go backstage to say goodbye after his performance.

He did good business the first time he came. He was a novelty. He came back again in 1981, but wasn't nearly as successful. He didn't do well at all, though at least he didn't use foul language the second time.

The problem was that with acts like his, our regulars got out of the habit of coming. That had been the secret to our survival. Some regulars came two or three times a week for the same show. Craig Russell and his ilk pushed the regulars out. When they weren't getting the proper show, the kind they liked, they started going to other restaurants. Sure, we did attract some new people with rock bands and more contemporary stars, but they came once and didn't come back. Meanwhile, the room had started to decline.

Wayland Flowers and Madame

It sank to a new low in October of 1983 when we had Wayland Flowers and Madame. Like Craig Russell, this puppet comedy act started in gay clubs, but had made more headway into the mainstream. The whole act consisted of Flowers, a ventriloquist, in conversation with Madame, a grotesquely ugly and flamboyant old woman done up in evening gowns and rhinestones. Flowers had had some luck appearing on the "Laugh In" program in the 1960's and made quite a few appearances with Marilyn McCoo on TV's "Solid Gold" and even on the "Hollywood Squares" game show in the seventies and eighties. Madame even had her own sitcom, "Madame's Place," the year before the act came to Toronto. You can't get more mainstream than that, I thought, so I wasn't expecting any trouble. Boy, was I wrong.

This was the most degenerate show I'd seen in my life. From what little I knew about Flowers and Madame, I was aware that double entendres and sexual innuendoes were a regular part of the act, but this was ridiculous. I never dreamed we'd have something like that in the Imperial Room. It was a total disaster. The language was awful. Every other word was some profanity. Myron Cohen never used one bad word and had people rolling in the aisles with laughter. Flowers went way beyond offensive.

I called a meeting the next day with Gino and the management. I said, "We've got to cancel this show. It'll destroy the room." They didn't have the guts. To anyone who called for a reservation, especially our regulars, I said, "Please don't come down." Some didn't call first, and we had families who only knew the act from TV walk out in horror.

I kept wondering, 'Why are we doing this?' This was the classiest place in North America. All we knew was class. We made it classy with the top stars. We tried to keep it that away with the talent, the service, the food, even the dress code.

Frank Gorsham

We had the pleasure of having Frank Gorsham, who at the time was very popular on stage, screen and TV. He was a very good actor and a great impersonator who could mimic Kirk Douglas and Burt Lancaster and became very well known on TV as the Riddler in the "Batman" series. When he appeared at the Imperial Room I found him to be very nice, but a little disturbed. Everything seemed to bother him; for example, someone coughing during his act or even going to the bathroom.

During the last night of his performance, while portraying King Arthur with a sword and dressed as a knight, on a Saturday night with a full house, a little over half of the show was completed when he heard someone in the audience whisper. Frank immediately walked off the stage, leaving the rest of the show uncompleted. I went backstage and informed him of how angry I was, especially since I was booking the entire room. I told Mr. Gorsham that he would never be welcome back to the Imperial Room. I left him in his dressing room. Needless to say, this was during the first show. We had to cancel the second and lost the revenue.

Months went by and I received a number of phone calls from Frank and his agent asking if he could appear again in the Imperial Room. His agent promised that we would never be embarrassed by Frank again. A month later, I had a spot that I could fill so we booked him. On opening day, I arrived at 3:00 p.m. for the rehearsal. The band was on stage and Frank was sitting at one of the rail tables. As soon as he saw me, he got up, approached me and gave me a big hug. I looked at him and said, "Tell me, Frank, what's going to bother you this time?" He apologized, telling me that he was going through marital and financial problems at the time, but it was all cleared up now. He thanked me again.
Needless to say, I always liked Frank and at the end of the week I approached him, asking if he would stay for three days to entertain at our big convention. He said, "Louis, because of you, I will stay three days." We shook hands and he honored us by staying longer.

I was saddened when he passed away. He was a good artist.

Stars of the Screen, Big and Small

Ginger Rogers

It was a great thrill for me when Ginger Rogers appeared in the Imperial Room in February, 1976. Naturally, I was big fan of all her movies, not only the musicals she did with Fred Astaire and other leading men, but also her dramatic roles. She was a very talented woman.

She had eight or nine people with her in the act, dancers who could take some of the focus off Ginger herself, who was moving a little more slowly than people remembered. But then she was 65 at the time, and for someone of that vintage, she moved pretty well indeed, singing and dancing away for almost an hour. I had the pleasure of escorting her on and off the stage, though in a way it was sad to see her up close and so old. The audience was far enough away that they could still see the image. But she was a lovely and classy lady, and our audiences loved her.

Alexis Smith

Back in the forties and fifties, I saw a lot of movies with Alexis Smith. She was never a major star, or even a great actress, but she co-starred with some of the greatest actors of all time, such as Cary Grant, Errol Flynn, Humphrey Bogart, Clark Gable, and William Holden. I thought she had pretty much left show business after around 1960, but I was wrong. She acted on stage with her husband, Craig Stevens (TV's "Peter Gunn") and won a Tony award on Broadway in 1971, a pretty good comeback for someone who'd been in the business for thirty years.

She came to the Imperial Room in 1975. Not many people remembered her, but she put on a low-key, pleasant show. She was still a tall and beautiful woman, with a nice voice and a good personality, and she left me a lovely note in appreciation of her run.

Tony Martin and Cyd Charisse

I was always a big fan of Tony Martin. I saw most of the musicals he made in the forties and fifties and still remember fondly his rendition of "Lover, Come Back To Me" in the movie "Deep In My Heart." I thought he was one of the greatest singers around, especially after he recorded "There's No Tomorrow" in 1959, which was based on my favorite, "O Sole Mio."

When he first appeared in the Imperial Room, he hadn't had a big hit since "Walk Hand in Hand With Me" in 1956 and his voice wasn't what it used to be. He needed a special microphone to be heard, but he did well. A great sax player from Toronto, Georgie Ault, was with him at that appearance.

The next time he came, he brought someone even better and well known -- the woman he'd married in 1948, Cyd Charisse. It was a real thrill for me to meet her. Like anyone else who loved movie musicals, I'll remember her great dance numbers with Gene Kelly in "Singin' in the Rain" and "Brigadoon" and with Fred Astaire in "Bandwagon" and "Silk Stockings." Tony was always a gentleman and Cyd was gracious and as lovely as ever. They worked together often in Las Vegas and put on the same terrific show in Toronto, though the audience numbers weren't anything to boast about.

As with other performers who didn't draw well, Tony's next Toronto appearance was at the Hook and Ladder Club in the north end of town. I went to see the show and was delighted when Tony made a big deal of the fact that I was there and his friend and I had treated him so well at the Royal York.

Gordon MacRae

Gordon MacRae was a big favorite of mine from the musicals he made in the 1950's, not only because of his great performances in "Oklahoma" and "Carousel," but also the many movies he made with Doris Day and other leading ladies earlier in the decade such as Shirley Jones.

After his film career was over, he was a frequent guest on TV shows and made a career playing nightclubs with his wife, Sheila. She was quite a star herself after appearing with Jackie Gleason on "The Honeymooners." Their daughter, Meredith, a lovely girl, was also very talented and appeared at the Imperial Room in 1972.

Gordon was supposed to perform on New Year's Eve in 1978, but got stuck by a storm in Chicago. We brought in Don Harron and Catherine McKinnon to fill that spot, and Gordon came to perform New Year's Day. He was a very nice guy and his baritone voice was still powerful, though not what it had been in the early days. Sadly, his long struggle with alcoholism had done some damage and probably contributed to the stroke he suffered a couple of years later. He died much too young.

Raquel Welch

Booking Raquel Welch in 1976 raised a few eyebrows. Everyone was familiar with her acting, her looks, and her image. But everyone said, "What can she do in a nightclub?" I wondered myself. But when she came out on stage, she was electrifying. She had backup singers and dancers, loads of energy, and glamour that lit the place up and filled it to the rafters every night. She was fabulous. Her energy didn't let up after she left the stage either. She had a number of parties for her staff, and always made sure I was invited. She was sociable, though also untouchable; she would cringe if anyone touched her.

I was one of the few to see her nightly transformation from merely pretty to glamorous. Anyone who saw her during the day might note the passing of a rather attractive woman but might never have even recognized her. But every night, I would accompany her to her dressing room at 6:30 where she'd spend almost three hours getting ready for the show (she'd spend three hours getting made up and dressed for a TV interview). She was very cooperative during her run, and a real pleasure to work with. When she came on stage, she was electrifying.

One night, when the show had already started, I was having dinner with her manager at my table in a corner. Suddenly, the front doors opened and about ten or twelve leather-jacketed people, men and women, walked in. They looked to the left, saw an empty table over in the back behind a column, and sat down. Raquel's manager was stunned.

They were bikers who had been upstairs in the Canadian Room for a professional boxing match and, when they saw that Raquel Welch was appearing, decided to barge right in. The staff suggested calling security right away, but I told them to let them be. I didn't want to see overturned tables and guests cowering in the corners. The bikers looked capable of just about anything.

I went to my desk and called both hotel security and the city police department. As the show ended, a small army of uniforms—about thirty policemen—appeared. I said, "Just stay on each side of the foyer to the dining room and we'll see what happens." I was gambling that the bikers would somehow pick up some of the aura of civility and class of the Imperial Room. When the show was over, the gang just applauded, got up, glanced menacingly around the room, and left, arrogantly but silently. None of the guests noticed anything amiss. One of my captains wanted to approach them and ask them to pay the cover charge. I said, "Leave them alone." Sometimes you're better off just doing nothing.

Florence Henderson

Florence Henderson made such an impact as the mother of "The Brady Bunch" on TV that many people forgot what a talented singer she was. After all, she toured the States as the lead in "Oklahoma," "The Sound of Music," and "Annie Get Your Gun" and appeared in many other musical productions on Broadway and elsewhere.

"The Brady Bunch" ended in 1974 and she "moved up" to the Imperial Room in 1975. She was a delightful, attractive lady who was nice to everyone—and we had a lot of families come in the week she was there—and she sang beautifully. Everyone enjoyed her.

Hal Linden

Hal Linden was such a popular favorite at the room, we booked him three or four times. Most people came simply because of the name recognition he achieved with his huge TV hit, "Barney Miller," so many people, including me, were surprised by how talented he was in other ways.

I discovered that he'd started out playing clarinet in a big band before moving on to Broadway. He'd appeared in quite a few stage musicals in the late fifties and sixties, he'd been a regular on the soap opera, "Search for Tomorrow," and had even made some movies before he made it really big on television.

He was a very nice man and a thorough professional. He put on a great show. He sang, he danced, and he played his clarinet. He even created a little scene from "Man of La Mancha" where he sat down in front of a mirror to make himself look like Don Quixote. Audiences loved him.

Barbara Eden

Barbara Eden made several movies and starred in another television series, "How to Marry a Millionaire," before she landed the role in "I Dream of Jeannie" that made her famous. It was a very popular show in the last half of the sixties, so when we booked her into the Imperial Room, she filled up the place most nights. But none of her roles, either in movies or on TV, had anything to do with music. It showed. She wasn't a great singer. Her voice wasn't all that interesting or powerful, but she did okay with a song.

She was a delightful woman though, very friendly and sociable. She told me she had signed a $50,000 buyout for appearing on Jeannie, and never got any residuals, despite the show being in re-runs for years. Luckily, I got to know her boyfriend too, who was with Magnavox. When I told him I needed a good TV set for my Florida condo, I got a hell of a good deal.

Leslie Uggams

Leslie Uggams was a beautiful woman and one of the most talented entertainers around. She was very professional, not surprising since she'd been working in show business since she was six years old.

She had made a name for herself on the TV show, "Sing Along With Mitch," and later had her own musical variety television series. She worked on Broadway too, and won a Tony Award in 1968. We had her in 1973, when her fame was at its height. She put on a fabulous show, and it was always a pleasure having her in the Imperial Room.

Joey Heatherton

Joey Heatherton became a pretty big star, mainly on television, in the 1960's. She had a personality and style that was right for the times, a blonde sex kitten in mini-skirts, making suggestive remarks and giving off fetching looks. She was never a really big star. She worked a bit on stage and made a few forgettable movies, but had her biggest success as a singer and sometime dancer. She had talent, but her personal life was a disaster, starting with a scandal with her marriage to a football star and going on to other difficulties I didn't know about when we booked her for an appearance in 1975. She had a television show during the summer of that year, but one that was very short-lived. We were warned that she would cause problems. There were.

The day she arrived, she demanded that an obscure make of mattress be installed in her suite. We couldn't accommodate her, and she moved to another hotel. She demanded a string section, so we booked 26 musicians, much more than the dozen we usually had. She was there for one week and every night she complained, loudly, about the sound, embarrassing the sound men from the stage. She did good business and we were sold out for the weekend, but the complaining was getting on everybody's nerves, especially mine. I suggested cutting back on the musicians if she felt the sound was overpowering her voice.

After a few nights, a fellow named Fisher, who seemed to be her drummer, manager, and boyfriend, all at the same time said, "Louis, we're canceling the show. I'm not going to risk ruining her million-dollar voice."

I thought he was being inflammatory. I took him backstage. "This is going to be very embarrassing for you and for us. You can't do that. You want her to sing just with a piano, I don't care. But let's stay focused here."

He said, "Okay, Louis. You're family."

We never invited her back, and few other people ever booked her after that time either. Her problems got worse and worse, and what was once a promising career was destroyed.

Sonny and Cher

I had got to know Sonny Bono pretty well when he played the Imperial Room with Cher in the early seventies. Sonny would come to check the sound system every afternoon and we'd always talk. We became close enough that we started calling each other "Gumbar," an affectionate Godfather-sort of name.

I also felt comfortable enough to make a slight criticism of their performance. In their first show, I thought there was too much talking and not enough singing. A few of the guests complained to me along the same lines. I brought it to Sonny's attention. He appreciated my concerns, so he and Cher took five minutes of dialogue out of the act and added another song.

In November of 1975, not long after he and Cher broke up, he came back as a solo act, although he also brought their daughter, Chastity, who was about ten years old at the time. He worked her into the stage act, showing home movies of her and the family. It was an unusual show, but I thought it worked well.

Louis and Sonny

Sonny was such a nice guy, always ready to please the audience and sign an awful lot of autographs for his many, many fans. I liked him so much that when he was in town and came to see a show one weekend dressed in an air force jacket, I actually let him in. For me, this was a big concession. He broke the rules, but, hey, it was Sonny. Gumbar.

On another occasion, I didn't notice any problem with particular guests, but the artist let me know in no uncertain terms what I had to do. Sonny and Cher were performing, giving a fabulous first show on the last night of their engagement. They were so popular that some people were paying the double cover charge and staying for the second show. We were ready to go, but Sonny and Cher did not come out. I went backstage, but didn't want to knock on their door. Maybe there was something going on between them that I shouldn't interrupt. I didn't know what was happening. No one else knew what was happening either. By about twenty to twelve, I had to do something. I knocked and said to Sonny, "Hey, Gumbar, what's the matter? What's wrong?"

"We're not going out until you get rid of two tables."

"What are you talking about? What tables? Come and show me." He pointed through the curtain to some regular guests seated very near the front. I said, "Sonny, I know these people. They're paying a double cover charge. They love you and Cher."

"I don't care. They have to go."

Then he told me that while Cher was singing "Danny Boy" during a quiet part of the ballad, she heard someone from one of the tables whisper to someone at the other table, "Look, Esther, Cher doesn't have any tits." (This was before she had breast implants, and she was wearing a see-through top.)

I went to the table and brought the situation to their attention. They gave me a very hard time, but eventually I convinced them to leave. I said, "There are 400 people behind us watching. I know this is very embarrassing. But the show won't go on. Don't worry about your bill. I'll look after it. Go next door to the Gazebo and have anything you want. I'll look after it." I filled up the table and the show went on.

Years later when Sony and Cher had split up, Cher performed a one-woman show at the then O'Keefe Centre. She would phone me every night and ask if I would meet her in front of her private elevator and escort her to her limo. I have had so many thrills but this was one that really stood out — me walking side by side with the great Cher.

"Louis Jannetta stepped into the world of the stars himself with small roles in Gladiator Cop; Night Heat; The Undertakers Wedding and GT the sequel to Gladiator Cop."

"Louis Jannetta is being arrested from Scott Hyland and Jeff Wincott in "Night Heat""

Chapter Five
Nothing Lasts Forever

From my point of view, it's not too hard to pinpoint when the Imperial Room started to decline as the room of the stars. As the 1970's ended, new management took up position in the hotel. Gordon Cardy moved on to become the chairman of all CP hotels and he asked Chuck Burton to come back as general manager. I liked Chuck, especially since he had been instrumental in making me Maitre D' back in the sixties. But I soon discovered our ideas on how to keep the room going were very different.

I could understand some of the decisions he made as the Royal York geared up for its 50th anniversary in 1979. He was quoted in the newspaper saying, "I think it's important we get away from this idea of the hotel being an old lady. If it is a lady at all, then she's a vibrant lady… We have spent a great deal of time in the last year reassessing our position in the market... We want to appeal to a wider range of people in the Imperial Room. That's why we're bringing in Sister Sledge, though we'll continue with people like Tony Bennett. One of the things you have to do in the hotel business is keep a maximum number of people interested in your property."
The traveling public was changing. Hotels were changing. He decided to not keep pursuing the convention crowds, believing they only came back every five years or so. He wanted to appeal to traveling business people and tour operators who could keep pumping people in. That was fine by me. But the secret of our success in the Imperial Room was the patrons, mostly from Toronto, who were regular guests who came back month after month, week after week, and sometimes night after night for very special performers. Burton spearheaded a regime that started to drive those regulars away.

The first thing he did was break up the committee that decided which acts would play the room. He developed a relationship with Gino Empry and named Gino the entertainment director, giving him control over who would be appearing. At first, I didn't object too much. We'd had our differences over the years, but I admired Gino as a publicist who had worked hard to generate coverage of our shows. I could book acts on a handshake and thought Gino could too. But Burton was very flamboyant and wanted to be very much involved in booking himself. To my mind, he and Gino made some very poor choices that diminished the stature of the room and tarnished its reputation.

When Mr. Burton managed a hotel for Canadian Pacific in Curaco in the early 1980's, he developed a relationship with a singer named Mark Anthony (not the salsa-singing Marc Anthony superstar who married Jennifer Lopez). He asked me to book Mark into the Imperial Room, but I'd seen him perform at the Sheraton Hotel in Toronto. He was a lounge act, not a star of the quality we had. I told Mr. Burton that I'd do the best I could to book him if he wasn't too expensive and there was space available. But I never did anything about it.
When Mr. Burton came back to the Royal York as general manager some years later, the first thing he did was book Mark Anthony with a contract for three dates. I couldn't do anything about it. Mark was a very nice guy and had a nice voice, but wasn't even close to being right for the Imperial Room. He didn't draw more than thirty or forty people a night. He was a disaster the first time he appeared and the turnout was just as bad when he came back the second time.

I couldn't bear to suffer his third engagement. I had developed a kidney stone and was getting attacks every once in a while, so I thought I'd have the operation to remove it, which in those days was an elaborate and painful surgical procedure. But I figured it would be a bigger pain for me to stay and listen to Mark sing to an almost empty room. I'd rather be in the hospital.

The operation was scheduled for a Monday morning, the same day Mark was to open. But Sunday night, after my wife and the priest had left, by some miracle, I passed the stone. As I checked myself out the next morning, my doctor joked that I'd "beaten him for two hundred and fifty dollars." I immediately went to the Royal York and booked a flight to Florida for Corinne and me. I wasn't going to stay around. My assistant could look after the room while I was gone. As I was making the arrangements at the travel counter downstairs, I bumped into Mark getting ready to rehearse. He gave me a hug and said, "Nice to see you again, Louis. I'll see you upstairs."

I said, "Have a wonderful time, but I'm going south." That was the last time I saw him. His third run was another disaster. He never did go on to headline any big rooms.

Another milestone in the room's decline came in 1982 when Gino convinced management to bring in a summer show, a Las Vegas-type magic show for tourists. Las Vegas Illusions came complete with topless show girls and a male stripper. When that word got out, so did the headlines in Toronto's newspapers: "Grand Old Lady goes topless." and "Imperial Room Bares Its Breast."

As the Toronto Star put it: "Another bastion of good taste will topple with the Royal York's decision to feature topless dancers this summer in its traditionally upright Imperial Room."

A lot of our guests weren't happy, and they let management know about it. One letter from the president of a prominent Bay Street company was typical. He wrote to Gordon Cardy, then the chairman and president of Canadian Pacific Hotels, that, having seen the newspaper article:

"I find it necessary and my obligation to write this letter. To think of such tasteless entertainment in the Imperial Room, whether or 'not total nudity,' destroys the image of the Imperial Room which has taken many years and so many dedicated and hard-working employees and entertainers to cultivate.

"I realize how difficult it is to operate profitably in our oppressed economic times, but to short sell the high-standing reputation of one of Canada's truly Grand Hotels is nothing short of prostituting the Grand Old Lady."

Management received many more complaints that somehow were ultimately attributed to me. It wasn't an unfair charge. I made a suggestion or two here and there. I confess I was a real jerk to the people that wanted Illusions to appear. I eventually received a letter from Chuck Burton that wasn't too complimentary.

I have received considerable correspondence and telephone conversations concerning the summer show. It is obvious from the letters and telephone conversations that much of the confusion surrounding the summer show is emanating from you. I find this strange and unnecessary. Your personal feuds with Gino Empry do not interest me... The Imperial Room needs all the support it can get. It does not need inside criticism and the sooner it stops the better we benefit, including you.

Once the show was up and running, I did everything in my power to make it successful. I wrote Burton back to tell him so. But all the letters added quite a bit of poison to Gino's and my relationship. He hated me for it, and he tried to cast a dark shadow about me to the Las Vegas group. But I treated them as well as I treated all our artists and I had a great party for them at my home in the country. They came to love me, but the relationship with Gino did not end that well.

Frankly, the show wasn't all that bad and did pretty good business. But it still brought down the room. So did a number of other summer shows like Ecstasy on Ice that featured topless skaters. It did fairly good business too. We had revues like Pulsations, with aerialists dangling above the dinner tables while the show girls danced, this in what was widely regarded as a bastion of elegance and refinement, the jewel in the crown of the Royal York, which was itself the crowning glory of the CP chain. It was depressing. All I could do was shake my head and keep doing my job. Many times I felt like weeping.

As I tried to keep the room first class, the war with Gino went on. I told him angrily many times, "Look what you've done. How can you book an act like this? You're destroying the room."

One day, I got a memo from Gino asking my advice on how to keep people from going backstage. It contained many criticisms, implied and otherwise, of how I did my job. I saw that it had been copied to Hans Grubmayr, the hotel's general manager at the time. I didn't even finish reading it. I rolled up the paper and, right in front of James Brown, who was rehearsing that afternoon, threw it in Gino's face. I said, "Don't you try to be some kind of big shot over me." Then I chased him out of the room.

Another time, he started arguing with me at my desk, using terrible language, over who was paying the costs of extra lights we'd brought in for the McGuire Sisters. I said, "Don't you use foul language at the front door of the Imperial Room." He told me to go f… myself. I was going to punch him right in the nose, but didn't.

The day after the Kids in the Hall fiasco, which Buddy Greco helped us through, I received a nice note and a handsome check from the chairman of the board, Gordon Cardy, who had also been in the audience that night, thanking me for how I handled things. Not so pleasant the next day was the word that, for Howard Cable, who was as distressed at the room's decline as I was, the Kids disaster was the last straw. He immediately submitted his resignation after twelve years of giving us the best band in town.

Things went from bad to worse. To a certain extent, the good talent was getting too expensive. I could understand bringing in groups and shows to make up for the void of the big stars. But the questionable acts kept coming. I just about had a fit in 1987 when I heard Gino had booked Carol Pope.

Personally, I liked Carol. I always treated her royally when she came as a guest. I always gave her respect. I brought her backstage to meet Tina Turner. But her act was raunchy and crude. As the singer with Rough Trade through the seventies and eighties, she was known as the "bitch goddess of Canadian pop." The kind of act she had was all leather schlock and shock that involved insulting people and swearing.

I called a meeting and said this was terrible. It was impossible. "She doesn't belong here and I don't want her here." This time I had some sway. We cancelled, saying we had to make repairs to the room. In retrospect, I wish she had come. She felt she had been "screwed around." She said she'd built a new act around the Imperial Room date and had spent substantial money. The next thing I knew, along with the Royal York and the CP Hotel chain, I was sued for $100,000 and Gino for $50,000. The suit never went to court. End of Story.

A couple of years after that, the end came for the Imperial Room as I'd known it and as I always wanted it to be. The Royal York announced that the room was going to once again become a dining-and-dancing palace, complete with Jackie Rae's 19-member Spitfire Band. It took me back to the old days of Horace Lapp and Moxie Whitney, though Jackie would gag at the comparison.

The last performer we had, on New Year's Eve 1988, was Peter Noone, formerly of Herman's Hermits. He was a very nice man and a fine entertainer. The night really marked the passing of the nightclub era that had seen the golden days of the Empire in Chicago, the Waldorf, Persian Lounge, and Rainbow Room in New York, as well as a few others. We'd outlasted most of the great rooms by ten years, but we were still an anachronism. Only supper clubs in places like Atlantic City and Las Vegas could keep offering big names because gambling could pay the bills.

Peter Noone

I wasn't the only one feeling nostalgic as the Imperial Room closed as a star venue on January 1, 1989. Many entertainers reflected on the loss in the newspapers of the day.

Hal Linden, who had appeared several times, took the long view, saying, "Younger clienteles grew up on rock acts and they don't really fit into a place like the Imperial. There may be something anachronistic about the place, but it's also kind of wonderful. There are no places that big where you can have an audience that close at hand. The Imperial was indeed the last of its kind. I'm sorry to see it go."

Peggy Lee was sorry too. She said, "I hoped they might change their mind. I don't know why they're closing it. Whenever I've been there we've had great business and a wonderful time. I think they'll soon feel the loss of excitement. It's a matter of class. It's an elegant room and they should have top acts there. We shouldn't lose our heritage. Audiences were wonderful, and we shouldn't lose that kind of rapport."

Ella, bless her heart, said the room was "like home. It was the kind of audience I felt comfortable with. Certain people from London, England, would ask for certain tunes and it was the same with people from Israel and Germany. It was like a United Nations. The people paid attention, the bands were always on top, and I never had to worry. You never had the dishes rattling or heard the people talking too loud, so you never got nervous."

For obvious reasons, I thought the most touching tribute came from Tony Bennett when he talked about all the good times and said how much he would miss the legendary Imperial Room. "The only room that came close was the Empire Room at the Waldorf. But it didn't have Louis Jannetta."

Rock 'n Soul

Paul Williams

Paul Williams had quite a good reputation in several fields. As an actor, he performed in an awful lot of movies over the years, and guest-starred on many television shows. But he made his mark mainly as a singer and, especially, as a songwriter. His tunes were big hits for The Carpenters ("We've Only Just Begun" and "Rainy Days and Mondays") and Barbra Streisand ("Evergreen," which also won him an Academy Award) and even Kermit the Frog ("The Rainbow Connection"). Singers like Sinatra and Ella recorded his songs too. He had his own hit with another of his compositions, "Old-Fashioned Love Song."

He was a talented guy and a small man, about five feet tall. He was troublesome. He seemed a little mixed up, maybe from smoking too much (and I don't mean tobacco). He wasn't always very nice to the audience. He used foul language and sometimes cut his act short. I heard many people as they walked out saying, "What a terrible show." But he did reasonably good business and, in what I thought was a very nice gesture, he put on an extra show for the hotel staff.

Jerry Lee Lewis, Host Patti and Ronny Hawkins

When we considered booking Jerry Lee Lewis into the Imperial Room in 1987, some objections were raised because of all the scandals that had surrounded him during his career, dating back to his marrying his 13-year-old cousin about thirty years younger and carrying on with stories about drugs and suspicious deaths among his wives. But he was a big star and we looked forward to having him.

It didn't seem as if he had slowed down at all over the years. His performances were as lively and unpredictable and as exciting as they'd always been, with him pounding away on the piano and singing up a storm. We had a great week with him. Ronnie Hawkins and many other stars came to see his show.

But he had a very bad habit of coming on late. Most guests were willing to put up with it, but one night we had a touring party of thirty or forty from England who were on a schedule and had to leave before Jerry decided to show up. They were very upset and, reasonably enough, refused to pay the cover charge since they didn't see the show. They were treated royally as far as the food and service went, but unfortunately, their anger got the better of them and they took it out on the staff.

James Brown

I was never a big James Brown fan. I didn't know much about his music, whether from his early gospel days or during the time he was making an impact in the world of rhythm and blues, soul, funk, and beyond. But it was almost impossible for anyone alive in North America in the mid-sixties not to have heard his two big 1965 hits, "Papa's Got a Brand New Bag" and "I Feel Good." They were just in the air everywhere and stayed there for decades. James' reputation as a performer was out there in the same way, even after his star status diminished a little bit in the seventies. People who weren't even fans, me included, just knew he was great.

I may not have had the expertise to know whether he deserved the titles of "The Godfather of Soul" or "Soul Brother Number One," but after he came to the Imperial Room in October of 1983, I could testify to his being "The Hardest-Working Man in Show Business." He put on a great show. His trademark antics on stage—with all his shrieks and screeches and bouncy dance moves—got the audience excited and energized in a way that wasn't all that usual for an Imperial Room crowd. He filled the place every night.

After his last show, I was having dinner at about three in the morning. The doors opened and I heard, "Louis, my man. I've been looking for you. I wanted to thank you."

I said, "No, thank you, James. You did great business and you were a pleasure to work with. I hope you come back again." It was also a pleasure that, as he shook my hand, he gave me three one-hundred U.S. dollar bills.

Decorum or the Night I Turned Bob Dylan Away

The Imperial Room always set the standard for elegance and class. This was a standard I worked hard to maintain in all my years as Maitre D'.

Many things changed since the days when almost all guests in the room dined and danced in tuxedos and gowns, but I tried to keep up many of the traditions I'd seen first hand since 1942. The dress code—jacket, shirt and tie for men—was one traditional expression of the standard. After all, guests weren't going just anywhere. They were coming to the Imperial Room for a fine night out. As long as someone was dressed appropriately, I'd make the best table available. Leisure clothes gradually became acceptable, but I always drew the line at jeans, t-shirts, and running shoes.

Some people gave me grief when I wouldn't let them in. It was often a problem on our "gypsy nights" when we let all the artists from the city's theaters in for the second show without a cover charge. It was difficult for me because they'd come in their work clothes, lining up outside the doors as some of the well-dressed 400 guests from the first show passed a disheveled crowd on their way out. I always imagined their opinion of the room dropping as they passed by. I kept a lot of jackets on hand for just such occasions. Some artists and stage hands refused to wear them at first, but when I wouldn't let them in, they eventually accepted my offer. They wanted to see the show.

One incident in 1986 became quite celebrated in Toronto. Texas country singer Tanya Tucker was performing when a guy turned up alone at the door wearing a parka, plaid shirt, worn jeans, and boots. He looked like a bum. I said, "I'm sorry, sir, but we have a dress code here and if I let you in it might offend some of our patrons." He didn't argue. He simply asked if he could sit down just outside the door and listen to the music. "Go right ahead, sir. Thank you." Tanya's parents saw him sitting there and, recognizing Bob Dylan as I did not, took him upstairs to dress him properly.

Once we started booking the top stars, another tradition became important: maintaining decorum among all the guests, for the sake of both the artists and the other patrons. After all, people came and paid good money to see great entertainers and deserved to be able to do so undisturbed. The artists themselves deserved proper attention and respect. I never let anyone bother the big stars, whether they were performing or simply dining. Most of the Imperial Room's clientele understood the rules and abided by them. But on some occasions, an inconsiderate or just plain miserable guest ignored them.

Kaye Ballard

Some artists had their own ways of dealing with what they considered disrespect. The great comedienne, Kaye Ballard, was irritated by someone at a table of ten down front while she performed. A woman—as it turned out, the wife of a Canadian Pacific marketing executive—sat with her back to the artist. I didn't notice it. The party paid their bill and left. Kaye chased them all the way to the lobby, loudly chastising the woman for not looking at the show. After that, I made sure whoever was down front paid attention. Sometimes, I turned them around personally.

Other artists looked to me to keep things in check, which I naturally did anyway. From my desk at the door, I could see every one of the 150 tables and could sense if something was wrong. A newspaper article once referred to me as the "Toscanini of the Room" for the way I orchestrated the staff and guests and stars. It helped that I knew eighty percent of the people coming to the Imperial Room. It was a steady clientele.

Rita Moreno didn't think too much of my conducting skills during one of her performances. A party of four came in nicely dressed and I sat them four or five rows from the front. After a few drinks, they started talking in such a way as to interrupt the show. It was always embarrassing for both me and the guests if I had to go close to the front and make a scene, even if I tried to do it discreetly. I made a few moves toward the unruly guests, but every time I started, they stopped talking, so I held back. I knew Rita would be upset, but I knew I might make things worse. Some artists on stage can control things like that themselves. In some places in New York, security would have come and just taken the guests out. I decided to leave things alone. After the show, Rita rushed up to me, saying, "You should have got rid of that table." She berated me for some time. I didn't speak to her the rest of the week, but after her last show on her last night she came to my desk, hugged me, thanked me for the week, and even allowed that I had done my best. For years afterward, whenever she was in Toronto for any reason, she always came to see me.

Rita Moreno

Usually, a discreet word was all it took to quiet patrons down, and I delivered many such words over the years to all kinds of guests, no matter who they were. While I was always loyal to our patrons, the star was the star, and if there was a problem, I didn't care who the patron was.

One night, King Carlos and Queen Sophia of Spain were at a table of six, with several Spanish generals at another table nearby. I thought the king and queen were louder than they should have been. Rather than approaching them directly, I went to the generals, spoke to them in Italian, and asked if they could please tell their Royal Highnesses to keep their voices down while the show was on. They did.

One night when Tony Bennett was singing, Don Curtis, the chairman of Canadian Pacific Hotels, was doing a deal to buy a hotel in Philadelphia, a business negotiation which seemed to continue during the show. His voice was much too loud. I went over and said, "Mr. Curtis, would you please keep your voice a little lower during this particular number." Mr. Curtis, who was not a fan of mine in the beginning, was very upset. He said, "You might have just lost a million-dollar deal for us. You be in my office tomorrow morning at ten o'clock." I immediately spoke to the hotel's general manager, Gordon Cardy, about the order. He said, "Forget about it."

After the show, I took Mr. Curtis backstage to meet Tony Bennett. I told Tony what had happened, and he suggested that I leave the two of them together in his dressing room. Tony told him exactly what I did for the Imperial Room and why performers appreciated it. After Tony spoke to him, Mr. Curtis, who had wanted to fire me several times, got to know who I was and became one of my best friends.

During my time as Maitre D', I was very proud that I rarely had to raise a finger in anger and rarely had to physically eject a patron for unbecoming behavior. Diplomacy worked best, though that was often difficult with demanding patrons, especially those who seemed to think they deserved special treatment because of their position or celebrity.

One night, a long line of people waited outside the door to see a popular performer's late show. As I began calling the guests in through the front door, our publicist, Gino Empry, came in through a side door with writer, Barbara Amiel (later the wife of Conrad Black), actor (and Karen Kain's husband), Ross Petty, and another man I didn't recognize. Gino thought he could do whatever he wanted, other people be damned, and arrogantly said he wanted "his" table immediately. I motioned to the door and said, "Do you see that line?" I directed Gino and his party to join the queue at the back of it. Needless to say, they were very embarrassed, but I wasn't about to let my regulars see other people butting in.

As the group left at the end of night, the man I didn't recognize gave me a dirty look and said, "I'm a journalist and you're going to hear about this." The next day, the Toronto Sun had a column by one of the paper's founders, Peter Worthington, headlined "The Bum's Rush." The article called me several nasty names and attacked my character, though in a backhanded way of explaining the circumstances, mentioned that my mother had just passed away, that I had gallstones and ulcers, and that all in all, there was obviously something terribly wrong with me. I didn't appreciate either angle to the story. I also never regretted my decision.

A similar situation arose when actors, Robert Culp and Bo Swenson, who gained some fame in the film, "Walking Tall," grandly brought six guests to the door to see Tina Turner's second show of the night. Culp and Swenson were wearing leather air force jackets, but I let that go by. They demanded a ringside table immediately. That I couldn't let go by, and explained that guests from the first show had not yet left.

They let me know, in a fairly obnoxious manner, that they thought I should just move somebody to suit their needs. I said the best I could do at the moment was a table on the first level in the center about halfway down the room. They took it, but after about 15 minutes, Bo came to my desk, brandishing a hockey stick he'd picked up at a hockey game at Maple Leaf Gardens earlier in the evening, and again demanded a table closer to the stage, adding, "And don't give me that shit." He was holding the stick like he held a baseball bat in "Walking Tall." I gave him a pleasant, but as steely a look as I could manage while gesturing to the still-full tables down front with one hand and taking the stick from him with the other. I said, "As you can see, no tables are free, but I'm sure I'll be able to accommodate you shortly. I'll return the hockey stick when you leave." He paused, but thought the better of making a fuss and went back to his table.

While I think I'm a gentle and generally affable guy, many people say I look like a wrestler or a big beefy bouncer. This always worked to my advantage. It helped sober up a few obnoxious drunks. Physical contact almost never happened, but you learn to expect the worst at any time and how to handle almost anything that comes up.

When Nelson Eddy was on stage just after we started booking the stars, a somewhat grizzled miner staying at the hotel on a long-term basis, came in every night. I was nice to the fellow all week long. I didn't make him pay the cover charge. On the last night, a sold-out Saturday, he snuck in without my knowing and found his own seat. I heard some noise, and there he was sitting in the back making such a ruckus he was interfering with the show. When I asked him to stop, he gave me such a hard time I called security. He was about seventy years old, but strong as a bull. We could barely control this guy, though eventually we got him out and back to his room.

PETER WORTHINGTON

The bum's rush

Life at the Toronto *Sun* has perceptibly changed since we added Patrick Conlon, Allan Fotheringham and Barbara Amiel to our star-studded array of non-conformist columnists.

I had anticipated problems from Conlon, since we got off to a shaky start, with him a bit over-anxious and me a bit testy. But he's settled down and is a gem. Well, *potential* gem, if he can keep away from politics which is catnip to columnists.

And Fotheringham is a delight, perhaps because he's often physically far away in Vancouver, or spiritually far away in Ottawa. And just because he can't spell Barbara Frum, Northrop Frye, gets confused between Chicago Mayor Jane Byrne and terrorist Kathy Boudin's roommate Susan Byrne, and writes vaguely libellous anecdotes about John Bassett, there's no reason to be upset. He is an uncomplaining joy.

Barbara Amiel has only been at the *Sun* a short time, but hasn't exactly blended into the woodwork. I was mildly amused when she teased (was it teasing?) June Callwood, with whom I often disagree but like. And Barbara managed to offend Lubor Zink, which wasn't easy because they tend to admire each other and fight the same dragons.

When Barbara wrote about the *Sun's* 10th anniversary party a surprising number felt Barbara had insulted my wife because she mentioned Yvonne spilling champagne on her $900 pantaloons, or whatever it is they are called. Sylvia Fraser, the author, called it good judgment on Yvonne's part.

Those $900 pants again

Amiel is the only person I know who wears $900 pants. While they looked spiffy enough on her, they kind of reminded me of the sultan's pants that Danielle wears. Same color too.

Robert Fulford buttonholed me at a brunch thrown by TTC chairman-cum-real estate speculator-cum-coin collector Julian Porter (who else?) and wondered with horror and relish if Amiel was so bankrupt of ideas that she was reduced to writing about *Sun* parties. Sylvia Fraser agreed.

Several complained about "poor June Callwood" having no platform from which she could respond to Barbara, which puzzled me since for 20 years June has never lacked a platform from which to wage all sorts of well-meaning mischief.

Which gets us to yesterday. I had been planning to write something really interesting about how nasty the Kremlin was, but along with the rest of the *Sun* staff got immersed in trying to find a home for Barbara's 10-month old dog which has curious black ringlets dangling all over it, is supposed to be a sheep dog and is Hungarian, which means it is charming company but, like Hungarian men, can be hard to live with. Or so I'm told. A Puli.

In between Barbara changing her mind about the dog, the staff tried to get its work done. Me too. Then Dan Proudfoot happened to mention that Barbara and two male companions got the bum's rush trying to crash Ronnie Hawkins' opening night at the Royal York's Imperial Room.

Two others phoned. "That's the sort the *Sun* attracts — getting tossed out of the Imperial room," said one fan.

With characteristic reticence Amiel didn't want to talk about it. Apparently she had been invited by impresario Gino Empry to opening night. She tried to follow Gino to the table. They were intercepted by someone Barbara describes as "a large, loud and quite terrifying *maitre d'* who didn't want us around." There were words, shouts, pushing and assorted antics. Apparently the Amiel party was told to get to the rear of the line. Gino was ignored and Barbara and her two escorts felt unwanted and were ejected.

"Maybe it was because my escort is of Albanian origin and the *maitre d'* is Italian?" said Barbara, ever-seeking a political or ideological explanation.

Maybe Barbara was dressed wrong. It seems she was wearing those $900 sultan's pants again which had miraculously recovered from their ordeal with Yvonne's champagne. And a tight gold sweater, like one that Barbara Frum has.

Mistaken for Frum, maybe?

"Maybe they thought I was Frum?" said Barbara.

I said I doubted it.

"Maybe the *maitre d'* knows June Callwood?"

"What were you doing at Ronnie Hawkins anyway?" I asked. "Do you actually like that stuff?"

"I used to watch him at the El Mocambo when I was in university. Nostalgia."

"Yes," I said, "He's been around a long time."

"Not *that* long," said Barbara, an edge in her voice.

Anyway it seems the story is getting better in the telling. One had her and her Albanian friend dancing on a table. "No," said Bill Scandrett, "that was Julian Porter — say, he'd make a great leader of the Tory party!" Scandrett is a fool.

I phoned Gino Empry and he more-or-less confirmed the incident. "We were all devastated," said Gino. "Barbara got a huge bunch of flowers for an apology and they want her to come in person as their guest so they can apologize properly."

"I'd like to see the next encounter," I said.

"You want to see Ronnie Hawkins?" said Gino.

"I don't want to get the bum's rush," I said. "I'm more delicate than Amiel." I was kidding. Gino didn't laugh.

"I tell you it was a mistake. Poor guy's mother recently died, he has gallstones, high-blood pressure and a bleeding ulcer. It's never happened before. Honest. When can you come?"

"I bet his blood pressure is higher today than yesterday."

Gino began apologizing again but I hung up — my phone was ringing; another well-wisher, no doubt, anxious to squeal on Amiel. It is great to be loved in Toronto.

Anyway, thats why my nifty column about the rotten Russians isn't in today!

Years later, I had more trouble with a prominent local businessman who regularly came to the Imperial Room. He was a fine gentleman when he was sober, but after a few drinks he always became very obnoxious and belligerent. I warned him several times. Finally, I told him he was no longer welcome and that if he showed up, I would stop him at the door. For the next three years, I received periodic phone calls saying, "Please, Louis, just give me another chance." Finally, I did.

The first few times the businessman came back, everything went fine. Then one night he came in with a party of eight. They were all beautifully dressed, with the businessman in a tuxedo. I still didn't trust him much, so I seated the party off to the side. It was Paul Anka's opening night. I introduced Paul to a standing ovation and when I turned to leave the stage I heard, "Booooo!" Paul's uncle ran out of the lighting booth, pointing the man out to me. I didn't have to be told who it was. I hustled to the table.

The man's bowtie was off and his collar undone. His wife was cringing. I leaned over and whispered, "What are you doing? Please, sir, don't you make another sound." Then I called security to be on standby. As soon as Paul finished his first number, the guy stood up and opened his mouth. Before he could let out another loud "Booooo," security had him up by his arms and out the door. I never allowed him back.

The same evening, a woman I knew well came in with a gentleman who had often come to the Black Knight Room. The woman always spoke too loudly, so I sat the couple far back from the stage. Not long after, a party of four arrived, one couple consisting of an older man and a young, tall, and very beautiful woman who wore a dress that left nothing to the imagination, cut so low in front that almost all eyes, male eyes anyway, were on her as the group made their way to a table down front. The four were eating their entrées when the loud woman from the back raced to the front, screaming and crying. She pulled the tablecloth off their table, sending wine, steaks, cutlery, plates, and glasses flying all over. The older man with the statuesque companion was her husband. We escorted her from the hotel. (They later made up and often came to the Imperial Room.)

Don Curtis, the CP chairman, happened to be in the audience that night and was appalled by what had happened, both with the boo-bird and the flying plates. As he would do at a Tony Bennett performance some time later, he said, "You be in my office tomorrow morning at ten o'clock." I called Mr. Cardy. "Forget about it."

Both incidents got my blood up. During Paul's show later in the week, two young guys were making a lot of noise and the people at the next table were very annoyed and upset. I grabbed the two of them, one in each arm. Big as I am, I've never been especially strong. But when the need arises, I can find some strength. I threw one guy down the steps to the foyer. By the end of the night, they apologized.

That kind of restraint wasn't in Shelly Berman's character. When the great comedian performed his phone monologues, we were almost sold out every night of the week. On Shelly's last night, the room was not quite filled when two very tall gentlemen from Buffalo came to the door. They were nicely dressed and looked sober. I sat them at one of the few remaining tables at the back. Everything was fine until halfway through the show. Then I could hear constant mumbling coming from their table. I went over and said, "Please, gentlemen, the show is on. Don't interrupt the show." But it didn't do any good. They kept it up. Every time they opened their mouths, I'd go over, always with the same result. Eventually, I told my captain to call security and I stayed beside their table. Every minute seemed like an hour.

Shelly Berman

Finally, the show ended. I saw Shelly walking towards their table and thought, "Oh, no." He picked up a pitcher of water on his way over and promptly poured the water all over their heads. Then he took them by the arms, escorted them out of the room, and went up to his own suite. For an hour after that, Shelly had me on the phone telling me how I should have handled the situation. He said I should have called them to the phone. I said, "Shelly, they didn't have a reservation. I didn't know their names." But I learned a lesson.

Family Matters

Maybe it was just because of my name or Italian background, but many people thought I had a relationship with some of the more dubious members of the Italian community. One of the Mills Brothers, Harry, even called me from Las Vegas very late one night to ask if I could recommend anyone to apply some muscle to some guy who was bothering one of his girlfriends. But that was never my scene.

Mills Brothers

I knew some of the figures who were well known to many people in the city of Toronto, but I only knew them as guests. People like Vic Cotroni, Paul Volpe, Albert Volpe, and Johnny "Pops" Papalia often came in, mainly to see Italian singers like Al Martino or Tony Bennett. Their characters were a little shady, but they were always friendly and polite and never did anything to embarrass me or anyone else. Some years later, when I had my own restaurant, Johnny "Pops" Papalia had a reservation for dinner, but he was gunned down in Hamilton before he could make it in.

None of the prominent members of the American underworld came to the room, or, if they did, I never knew about it. (One noted criminal, James Earl Ray, stayed at the Royal York after assassinating Martin Luther King Jr., and, we found out much later, had lunch in the Imperial Room.)

McGuire Sisters

There was one exception. In the mid-seventies, we booked Phyllis McGuire of the McGuire Sisters. She was a wonderful woman who I liked very much. The first day she was there, she came down early to make sure the sound system was okay and other arrangements were made. Then she went backstage. The room was still closed, but two gentlemen came to the door. One was a big black man who said his name was Parker. The other was a little guy wearing a hat and dark glasses. He said he'd like to see Miss McGuire. I noticed something a little different about them, not the least because Mr. Parker was carrying what I thought was a violin case. I wasn't exactly sure what it was, but it made me think of some of the Jimmy Cagney and Edward G. Robinson movies of my youth. I realized their importance from their manner. I took them backstage and knocked on the dressing room door. I said, "Miss McGuire, there are two gentlemen here who'd like to say hello."

She came out and said, "Oh, Sam," and hugged and kissed the smaller man. Then I knew for sure that this was Sam Giancana, the reputed crime boss of Chicago and, according to him, of Miami and Los Angeles as well.

After their greeting, he said to me, "Are you the boss?"

"I'm the manager of the room. I look after things."

He took out a hundred dollar bill, handed it to me, and said, "Here, make sure you look after her."

He stayed for four days and I kept aside a cozy corner for him and Phyllis. One night, I didn't know he and Mr. Parker were going to come in and we were full. I asked a long-time regular and friend, Irv Winston, if he'd mind letting them sit with him. Decades later, my friend still talks about that night.

Not long after that, I traveled with a group on my first trip to Las Vegas, which was very exciting. We went to see Johnny Carson perform, and I saw Phyllis, Sam, and Mr. Parker come in and be escorted to the front. I sent my card down and after the show, the three of them came over to our table and had a nice chat with me and my friends.

That, and winning $7,000, was the highlight of the trip (though the winnings were unfortunate in the long run, just feeding my gambling addiction).

Not long after, the McGuire Sisters performed in The Imperial Room. I went to Phyllis and said, "Miss McGuire, that was very nice of you and Sam and Mr. Parker to come by and say hello to my friends in Vegas."

She said, "Louis, I love that man." But not for too much longer, since Sam soon had several bullets in his head.

Orchestras

Nelson Riddle

Nelson Riddle was one of the most admired arrangers of the fifties and sixties. He put out a lot of his own albums, mainly of mood music, but was best known for backing singers like Dean Martin, Peggy Lee, and especially, Frank Sinatra. I had all those recordings, and so did just about everyone else I knew. He worked in movies and television quite a bit too, writing theme songs for some of the most popular TV shows.

By the time he came to us in 1981, he had pretty much retired, though he made a comeback a few years later with a recording of torch songs with Linda Ronstadt. He didn't bring any musicians with him. He just conducted his arrangements with the guys from Howard Cable's orchestra. He was a very nice man.

Mantovani

The Mantovani Orchestra made an appearance in the Imperial Room in 1987, about seven years after Mantovani himself had died.

I enjoyed Mantovani's music. I was probably predisposed to it because of his Italian roots. He was born Annunzio Mantovani in Venice, but moved to England when he was seven and never left. His light, easy-listening sort of music, with its "cascading strings," was hard to avoid in the 1950's and even into the 1960's. He turned out an awful lot of albums, mainly of movie and television themes. He sold well. In fact, before the Beatles arrived, Mantovani was the biggest selling British artist in America.

I thought he made beautiful music, soft and lush and pleasant, though a lot of people seemed to dismiss it as "elevator music" as time went on. The orchestra—with thirty musicians—traveled around the world trying to keep his style of music alive, which was kind of funny since performing live was something Mantovani almost never did after World War II. He built his whole career around recordings. The group still did have its fans.

Brain Mulroney, George Bush and Louis

Chapter Six

The Right Honorables

For decades, the Royal York Hotel was a home away from home for political figures from across the country. I got to know the premiers of just about every province, as well as all the prime ministers from the days of Louis St. Laurent in the late 1940's (except Kim Campbell and Paul Martin, though I knew his father, the Honorable Paul Martin, Sr.). I never met Mackenzie King, but St. Laurent and his son would often come to the Imperial Room for a nice quiet dinner.

John Diefenbaker frequently came with his wife, Olive, and Lester and Marion Pearson were also frequent guests. Their political parties didn't matter to me. I wasn't Liberal or Conservative. I just wanted to make sure they were well looked after. They were both very pleasant and we often chatted, especially about the Italian-Canadian hockey league.

I got to know Pierre Trudeau quite well because, almost alone among the prime ministers, he not only came in for dinner when he was in town, but also took in the shows for performers he was especially fond of. He couldn't see many since he was always busy when he arrived. One night I came down the steps from the Imperial Room as he was walking through the lobby with his entourage. He waved, so I approached him and said, "Good evening, Mr. Prime Minister. How nice to see you." We walked arm in arm to the elevators, with photographers all around. I said, "Why don't you go upstairs and relax a bit, then come on back down for the late show."

He said, "I'm sorry, Louis, but I've got a big meeting in the morning."

As he got on the elevator, I pointed my finger at him and said, "Oh, come on down, Prime Minister. You haven't been here since you saw Ella Fitzgerald."

Pierre Trudeau

The next day there was a picture of me pointing at him, with the headline, "Do you have a reservation?" I got a number of calls because of that picture, as well as a letter from Winston's Johnny Arena gently chiding me for getting caught in a gesture no Maitre D' should ever make, especially to such an important person as a prime minister.

John Turner was a regular at the Royal York during his time on Bay Street, when he became prime minister, and after he left Ottawa. At the Imperial Room, he always sat at Table 69A, the same table I used to have my dinner and survey everything that was happening in the room.

When he became prime minister and was upstairs preparing for his Christmas media interviews, one of the bellboys came to me and said Mr. Turner wanted to see me in the Royal Suite. As soon as the door opened, he got up from his seat across from the CBC's Peter Mansbridge and greeted me like an old friend. Even today, he often comes to the alumni meetings I attend every six months or so where the people who worked with me at the Imperial Room and who are now running most of the most prestigious clubs in Toronto get together to share old times. I felt a twinge of sadness when Brian Mulroney defeated him after Mr. Turner had so little time in office, though in the years after, Mr. Mulroney's famous charm worked on me as it did on so many others.

Former President Reagan & Pearl Bailey

Chapter Seven
Crowned Heads and Presidents

Many members of royal families and heads of state visited the Royal York Hotel over the years. I had the pleasure of looking after King Carlos and Queen Sophia of Spain and attending to President Luis Echeverría of Mexico in the early 1970's when they dined in the Imperial Room, making sure everything they needed was provided promptly and well. We prepared ourselves for weeks when we were informed that Princess Margaret would be coming with a party of six. When she arrived, I greeted her graciously and deferentially and escorted her to her table for dinner. She had a wonderful evening, enjoying both the meal and the entertainment, and on her way out she thanked me very much, which was a great honor for me.

My position at the hotel and in the city led to a number of other events at which I had the honor of being in the presence of the world's most prominent people. When Her Majesty Queen Elizabeth and His Royal Highness Prince Philip came to Toronto, the management asked me to walk around the Canadian Room in my white tie and tails, saying hello to people and making introductions for the special guests in attendance. Some years later, I had the great pleasure of being invited to a luncheon at the Sheraton Hotel for the Queen and her consort. I was also thrilled to be invited as a guest of the City of Toronto to a dinner of 200 people honoring President Giuseppe Saragat of Italy. The federal and provincial governments some years later invited my wife and me to a luncheon with Prime Minister Mulroney and another president of Italy. I took Jack Lonergan with me as my wife couldn't make it. When Mr. Mulroney spoke, he said there were many great Italians in the room and pointed out to the president that the Italians sitting before him had first built most of Toronto and now owned most of it.

Perhaps one of the most memorable evenings for me came at a dinner in the Canadian Room organized by Prime Minister Brian Mulroney to introduce the elite of the city to President Ronald Reagan, who was in town for a summit. I was the guest of John Bitove, of the Bitove Corporation, who had a private line to Prime Minister Mulroney's office, as he helped out however he could with fundraising for elections. Much to my surprise, while the elite people I knew from the Imperial Room were seated way in the back, our table was about ten feet in front of Mr. Reagan. Mr. Mulroney, who I knew quite well by then, smiled a number of times in my direction, and the President also looked over, often with a smile on his face and the famous twinkle in his eye, perhaps wondering who this guy with the funny hairdo was. It was a great night.

Vic Tomesicchio Sr., Johnny Lombardi, Beniomino Gigli, Louis, Mrs. Tomesicchio and Jerry Tomesicchio

Chapter Eight
New Beginnings

In January of 1989, as the new era at the Imperial Room began, a lot of people working in the hotel were terribly demoralized. The whole place had taken on such an unhappy atmosphere during the previous few months, and that atmosphere only got worse. The last six months of Gino's regime had hurt us badly with our patrons. New changes in concept and format hurt the staff almost as much.

I'd tried very hard not to let this state of affairs come about. In 1988, I had approached Robert DeMone, chairman of Canadian Pacific Hotels and Resorts, and suggested that, as the general manager of the Royal York Hotel and with a good executive crew, I felt I could bring the morale back up. Wherever I went inside the place, everyone from the janitors to the executives were always kind to me. I treated them all very well and they appreciated the respect I had for them. I also felt I could be an asset to the hotel in the greater community. Everyone in town always answered my phone calls, from newspaper reporters to politicians, company presidents to board chairmen.

He said, "I appreciate your wanting the position, but we're looking for someone with managerial experience."

They brought in Timothy Whitehead from Ottawa, who had been manager of the year at one of the hotels he was running at the time. He doubled my salary and gave me free parking so I would stay and run the Imperial Room and teach the staff our new concept. I liked him. But he was always talking about "the winds of change," a phrase he used constantly. He certainly changed a lot of things besides taking all the entertainment out of the Imperial Room and reverting to ballroom dancing. To me, dancing was a one-night-a-week situation. I always maintained that if Guy Lombardo couldn't fill up the Imperial Room, as he couldn't the last few times he was there in the mid-seventies, who could? Whitehead had also gotten rid of all the lights and sound systems, despite my objections that we'd need them for private functions if for nothing else.

But he had even more changes in mind. Whitehead, a new chef, George McNeil, and I were sent to New York to see what was happening in the trade there. When we came back, even more winds of change blew through.

We were going to change the kitchen to serve nouvelle cuisine, with everything cooked to order. George McNeil was a great chef and nouvelle cuisine was fine, but not for the huge Imperial Room. Advertising and marketing were going to be aimed at the birthday and anniversary crowd and feature the Spitfire Band. We were going to hire female servers for the Imperial Room. I didn't think that was a good idea, not out of any chauvinist feeling. I just knew how heavy the workload would be. Many young ladies applied, and I made sure to warn them how difficult it would be to carry huge trays with heavy silver covers back and forth to a kitchen that was far away from the tables. They all claimed they were very strong and could do it. Starting in January, 1989, we trained them for a month and a half, teaching them about the food, the wines, and the standards of service expected at the Imperial Room.

The official reopening took place on February 14 -- Valentine's Day. Senior executives and managers with CP hotels and the Canadian Pacific Limited chairman, Bill Stinson, came from Montreal and other cities for the event. Many regulars wanted to come, but I was only allowed to accept 50 outside reservations.

William Stinson, Louis & his wife Corinne

The evening turned out to be one of the worst disasters we ever had. Serving nouvelle cuisine, the kitchen couldn't possibly cope with 350 people. People waited and waited and waited for their food. Managers were very upset. Ivor Petrak, who worked as a waiter when I was young and who eventually made the Banff Springs Hotel very profitable, asked the food and beverage director of CP Hotels, "Whose idea was this? This is terrible."

At the end of the evening, Timothy Whitehead introduced the chef and me, both of us greeted with a warm round of applause. Then he told the audience that they were being used as guinea pigs. Managers were there on CP's ticket anyway. For all the other paying guests, the evening was complimentary. No one was charged.

The evening started a downward spiral of total unhappiness for me and many of the staff, as well as many guests. After a month and a half, all the waitresses, except for one very strong lady, had quit. The same month, one very prominent Bay Street stockbroker, who had been a regular noon-time patron for years, sent a letter to Tim Whitehead, saying he and his father had visited the room for lunch for the first time since the renovation "...and I wish to tell you it was an absolute, unmitigated disaster." He used to come five times a year for the evening shows, but would never return. "Now your food is marginal, your kitchen is inflexible, and there's no show. Given sufficient time, there won't be any patrons."

People were complaining the dance floor was too small, even though it was triple the size we usually had. They expected the whole room to be a ballroom. We brought in instructors to teach people how to ballroom dance. For me, the worst part of the new policy was that I was only allowed to accept 50 reservations in the period of an hour; an hour later, another 50. The room looked terribly empty. But even then, the guests were waiting for their food. People were terribly upset about the menu. One regular guest grabbed the food and beverage director by the neck and said, "What are you doing to this room?' It wasn't a happy atmosphere, and the corporate management recognized the terrible situation to the extent that Whitehead was moved out. Hans Grubmayr became general manager.

In June, I had my usual benefit for the Canadian Italian Hockey League in the hotel's Canadian Room. Mr. Stinson came down from Montreal. The guests were people who also came to the Imperial Room. It was a fun evening, as these events always were. I went on stage for my thank-you speech, during which I told them what was going on in the Imperial Room. I lied, telling them how wonderful it was now that we had ballroom dancing. They all booed.

That night, Mr. Stinson and I sat up until three in the morning. I didn't like to burden him with tales of so many problems during what was supposed to be a non-business night, but I sure wanted to unburden myself. And I did. Other people at the benefit had talked to him too, wondering how the management could do what they had done to the room.

The next day, Mr. DeMone came into the Imperial Room for lunch. Mr. Stinson had spoken to him. He brought me and Hans Grubmayr together to talk about what my plans might be for the room, considering the undeniable problems we had had the past few years. I told him I could understand some changes in policy. A lot of the artists were dying off. Some of the acts still around were costing $50,000 a week. But I had other ideas.

I suggested a big star like Tony Bennett, who was still doing night clubs, to re-open the place. Then, with a limited amount of artists available, have a revue for two months, then another star, then another revue. The weekends alone would pay for the cost of the revues. Hans, who was a great man, and I were in agreement that I would have full control of the room and do the booking.

He said, "Some people think you're going to make a lot of money."

I said, "If you don't trust me, tell me to go f... myself."

After the meeting, I was going to meet with Tony Bennett right away to ask him to commit to appearing. Then Hans told me to put things on hold. By early July, I was given the go-ahead "to present proposals for a new concept to deal with bringing the Imperial Room back to its financial success and its prestige as it was." With the opportunity to be involved, I felt twenty years younger. Within a couple of weeks, I submitted a proposal with facts and figures covering hours of operation, cover charges, menus, food and beverage costs, artist costs, service, staffing, advertising, management. I was asked for clarifications.

The summer dragged on with no progress. I had another meeting with Hans that wasn't as positive as I had hoped. I wrote to Bob DeMone, not only again pointing out that the present concept was not working and again offering my services as general manager, but also telling him that I felt there had been too many outside people brought in to the hotel in executive positions without knowing the Royal York itself. The finer qualities we were once renowned for were diminished and the staff increasingly felt that no matter how hard they tried to do their jobs well, it was never good enough for advancement. At the end of the summer, I wrote again to Bob DeMone. Still nothing happened. I was extremely unhappy. My blood pressure was skyrocketing and I did some very stupid things. At meetings, whenever discussion came around to the Imperial Room, I'd raise my voice and say, "Get it back to what it was!" I truly believed it was for the benefit of Toronto. The management was taking something away from people that had supported us all their lives. They had invested in the room and then suddenly, everything had come crashing down and they had lost all their privileges. I was beginning to feel physically ill much more often.

By this time, John Bitove had contacted me. His company was running the operation at Toronto's new SkyDome sports facility that had opened in the spring of 1989. He had big plans, but the first year had not gone as well as he or anyone else had hoped. He offered me a very handsome six-figure contract to be senior director of SkyBoxes, with a mandate to give the 161 private SkyBoxes at the Dome the same sort of high profile I had helped the Imperial Room achieve. Bitove figured my experience with the kind of corporate clientele he wanted to attract would come in handy. I sat on the offer for some time. The Royal York didn't know anything about it.

That fall, John Bitove was invested into the Order of Canada. I was invited to a dinner at the King Edward Hotel to celebrate the appointment. I expressed my thoughts to a few people there, like Steve Stavro, the owner of the Toronto Maple Leafs. He and several others said I should not leave the Royal York. They were quite insistent. After dinner and perhaps a bit too much wine, I was asked to go up front and sing a song by Rocco Marcello. I had the Bitove contract in my pocket. After I finished singing, I said, "I want you to know that after nearly 50 years at the Royal York Hotel, I'm joining the Bitove family."

I've done many stupid things in my life, but that was the stupidest thing I ever did. I didn't have enough intelligence to just let things go by. I immediately felt like a traitor. The Royal York had given me everything.

The news got out quickly. I was in the papers and on radio and television almost the next day. The hotel manager, Johann Isopp, summed things up pretty well when he was quoted in a newspaper saying that, "As we changed our format, Louis became extremely unhappy. The Imperial Room especially, he felt like it was part of his body."

When I started at the Dome in February of 1990, there was a picture in the paper of me out front of the Royal York, waving goodbye. Every time I looked at it, I thought, 'How could I have been so inconsiderate and selfish? That place was my life.'

They had a huge good-bye party for me in the Imperial Room that February, the first party ever given for a departing employee. I didn't want to have a party since I was already working at the Dome, but as one of the hotel's longest-working employees, I couldn't refuse. More than 500 people came to honor me and my family. It was a wonderful night, with lovely messages read out from managers of Canadian Pacific hotels across the country, from the Empress Hotel in Victoria to the Hotel Newfoundland in St. John's, from the Lieutenant-Governor of Ontario, and many, many others. The next month, I was back at the hotel with 800 guests at a $200-a-plate event, arranged mainly by Johnny Arena and friends, both to celebrate my birthday and to establish a Louis Jannetta Scholarship Fund, with half the money raised going to the Variety Club children's charities and half to Canadore College in North Bay, Ontario.

The Bitove Corporation organized a well-covered welcome luncheon for me at the beginning of February, suggesting I give a few upbeat remarks to the press about how the focus for entertainment in Toronto had shifted to the SkyDome and how five-star service was going to be the standard we aspired to. I put my all into it and tried to focus on the future.

But while I was at the Dome, I received a letter from a long-time Imperial Room regular, with a poem that makes me cry like a baby every time I read it. I felt like slapping myself, thinking, "How could I have been so stupid, leaving a place that was my whole life?"

At the Royal York the other night
We saw a sad, depressing sight.
The grand old Imperial Room
Was as silent as a tomb.

As we stood there in the door,
Two couples were dancing on the floor.
There was no laughter, applause or cheers.
Dead and gone were the glory years.

Where were the movers and the shakers,
The politicians, the money makers,
The Rosedale crowd and Forest Hill?
The music played but the room was still.

We stood there lost in the memory
Of the golden years, how it used to be
The finest place in town to go,
When Louis Jannetta ran the show.

Maitre D's, waiters, busboys too,
Worked as a team under you.
What a job you did and did so well.
For all those years in that hotel.

You brought in the stars who gave us pleasure,
Nights to remember, memories to treasure.
Lines of people stretched out the door
As you squeezed more tables onto the floor.

You knew all the faces, remembered the names,
Heard all the gossip, guessed all the games.
I remember how I used to say,
"I'd change places with Louis any day."

You met many people from every coast,
Like a wonderful party where you were the host.
You were the heart and soul of the place,
Who brought us the glamour, each famous face.

Marlene Dietrich who caused a sensation,
Her loyal fans gave her a standing ovation.
Tony Bennett who always drew a huge crowd,
As you stood in the doorway, you must have been proud.

Remember Craig Russell? I enjoyed the show
As he did Tallulah, Judy Garland, and Monroe.
We saw Raquel, Carol Channing, Bernadette too,
Connie Francis, Charo, all brought in by you.

Poor Rudy Vallee, although he tried,
His era was over, his fans had all died.
You made it all happen, the laughter, the tears,
The applause, the excitement, for many long years.

As this wonderful city started to boom
There was nowhere like the Imperial Room,
The place where the stars came, the fine ambiance.
Where else in Toronto could we see Ginger dance?

The curtain is down now, nothing's the same,
But the ghosts of the past in memory remain.
How sad for you, Louis, to watch it all fade,
The place you'd created, the room you had made.

Your job there was finished, time to move on.
The energy's missing, the crowds have all gone.
I'm glad we could share in the fun and the glitter.
Life's full of changes, no time to be bitter.

Louis, I've heard you have found a new home.
THE IMPERIAL KING IS NOW KING OF THE DOME.

All the best, Louis
In your new career
Margaret R.

The new career started well. I went to work early in 1990, getting things organized for the upcoming baseball season. I soon had very special guests. On April 10, Prime Minister Brian Mulroney and President George H. W. Bush held a day of talks at SkyDome, along with Canada's Minister of External Affairs, Joe Clark, and the American Secretary of State, James Baker. They had a nice dinner created by the Dome's Chef de Cuisine, Stephen Demichelis, at the very exclusive Founders Club, then moved on to the Blue Jays' SkyBox to watch the home opener between Toronto and Texas with Baseball Commissioner Faye Vincent and Bobby Brown, President of the American League. As the director of SkyBox services, it was up to me and my staff to look after them.

When they came in, Prime Minister Brian Mulroney had a Blue Jays jacket on and the President wore a Texas Rangers jacket since his son, George W., was one of the owners of the team at the time. I greeted them in my tuxedo. Mr. Mulroney introduced me to Mr. Bush and started telling him the story of my life, mentioning that I'd just left the Royal York after nearly 50 years. President Bush, a tall, strong-looking man, took the story in with a delightful show of interest.

They stayed in the box for a short bit, then went to do radio and television interviews and came back in civilian clothes. I was at the bar speaking to my hostess when the President got up from his chair, came over, put his hand on my shoulder and said, "Well, Louis, is everything going well?"

I said, "Yes, Mr. President, everything's going wonderfully well."

Pierre Bougain, Fairmont Royal York General Manager at the time

Johanne Hissop, Fairmont Royal York, Manager at the time

John Turner & Louis

As he asked for a soda water from my hostess, I was debating with myself on what to do about a baseball I had in my pocket, a ball I'd taken from a box of dozens of balls kept in the Dome box for special guests. I didn't want to be too brazen with a man I'd just met, especially one who happened to be the most powerful man in the world, but finally I thought, what the heck. I said, "Mr. President, would you please sign this ball for me?"

He said, "Louis, I'd be delighted to."

On the way out, Mr. Mulroney and President Bush thanked me for a wonderful evening. But President Bush turned to me and said, "Louis, thank you for a wonderful evening. But do me a favor. Would you see that the Blue Jays take it easy on Texas? I am sixty years old and my son has to support me now." George Bush at the time was owner of the Texas Rangers.

I asked him to sign it for my daughter, Susan, and explained she had had a terrible accident that February. She had just come out of a coma and was getting around in a wheelchair at a rehab hospital. He said, "Oh, Louis, I'm so sorry. My prayers will be with her." He signed the ball, "To Susan, Love George Bush," then took it over to have it signed by Prime Minister Mulroney, Faye Vincent, and Bobby Brown. (Some years later, Tony Bennett signed it and so did former Prime Minister John Turner, bringing the number of signatures to six.) It was quite a day. And the Jays beat the Rangers, 2 to 1.

It was a memorable start to what turned out to be a short stay at the SkyDome. Through the spring and early summer, life unfolded at a pleasant pace and in a very satisfying way. I enjoyed the work and many old friends dropped by to say hello, such as Bobby Orr and Alex Trebek, who I knew well from long before his Jeopardy days in the States. Alex interviewed me at the winter carnival in Quebec when he was first starting out. One day, as I was walking with my staff and busy giving them directions, a group of men walked by, but I took no notice of them. One of the hostesses later came and said, "Mr. Jannetta, you're wanted in the Blue Jays box." When I went in, Wayne Gretzky said, "What's the matter, Louis? You don't say hello any more? Didn't you see me?"

There were happy events outside the SkyDome, too. A major publisher, McLelland and Stewart, offered me a contract to write a book about my fifty years at the Royal York and signed up two writers to help me get my story in shape. The Toronto Transit Commission asked me up to do some television commercials about the virtues of TTC public transit. A restaurant owner planned some commercials that would feature me recommending his establishment. I was also honored when Fern Flaman, who was to be inducted into the Hockey Hall of Fame in the fall of 1990, asked me to accompany him to the Hall of Fame dinner, present him with his medal, and give a speech before 1,700 people. Most satisfying of all, several people, all members of the Order of Canada, called from Ottawa and elsewhere to tell me that I would soon be made a member of the Order, the highest recognition Canada can give, not only for my years at the Royal York, but for my 45 years running the Italian-Canadian Hockey League and my decades of charitable work with Variety Village, the Knights of Malta, and other organizations.

John D'Amico, Jack Lonergan, Louis, Bobby Orr & Ray Ferracuti

My World Crumbled

Part of my job involved visiting the Skyboxes to make sure the corporate tenants were being served in the best way possible. While visiting a suite owned by a prominent Toronto family, owners of a prominent business, I would often see a woman chatting and drinking with other people. It turned out she was a hostess hired by the family to entertain their guests. During the course of a few conversations, she mentioned she wanted to start her own catering business and asked if she could talk to me about the hospitality industry. We arranged to have dinner at the restaurant where I was doing some commercials and where the owner had invited me to be his guest. We had a productive dinner, some laughs, and some wine. I drove her home and being polite, escorted her to the front door. She thanked me for the help and for a great evening and said she'd see me the next day at the SkyDome.

But I didn't see her the next day or for some time after. Eleven days later, I was getting ready to attend a luncheon at the Royal York. The hotel was being honored with the Holiday Award, one of the most prestigious awards in our industry. At eleven o'clock in the morning, I received a phone call from a detective who said he wanted to come and talk to me. About a half hour later, two detectives arrived and informed me that I was being charged with sexual assault, and proceeded to read me my rights. I was stunned. I told them, "But the lady and I just had dinner at a restaurant."

They were very polite and nice enough to allow me to walk ahead of them as we left my condominium so I wouldn't be embarrassed if some of the people I knew saw me being frog-marched through the lobby. They took me to the police station where I was photographed, fingerprinted, and put in a cell. I was allowed to phone Michael De Rubies, a lawyer and good friend, who came down to the jail and took me home. Corrine was waiting for me, worried and heartsick. I told her I was very naive and wrong to have even agreed to meet for a business meeting with the woman, but assured her that nothing else had happened. Needless to say, the charge made for a monumentally sad day and a sleepless and sweaty night.

The next day, I returned to work. Oddly enough, the young woman had not returned to work 11 days later and had asked a staff member to have me go to the Skybox where she worked to meet some of the owners. I didn't think that was a very good idea.

I went to see Tom Bitove, head of catering at the SkyDome, and passed the news on to him. I told Tom I had done nothing wrong and would be vindicated, but that when the news hit the media, there would definitely be problems. A few days later, my situation was all over the newspapers and talked about on radio and television. I was devastated. It was obvious that I couldn't continue greeting people at the SkyDome in any kind of official public relations capacity when so many terrible newspaper articles had appeared, all referring to me as the "King of Hospitality." I resigned my job.

Much to my regret, I also called Fern Flaman to cancel my appearance at the Hockey Hall of Fame dinner. My name had already been printed on the menus for the event, but with all the bad publicity, I thought someone might say something embarrassing and possibly ruin the evening for Fern or others. The dominoes fell one by one. My TTC commercials were cancelled. The book contract was cancelled. The Order of Canada never arrived.

Given the seriousness of the charge, all that was understandable, though I knew I had done nothing wrong with the young lady. But I also knew the bad publicity had embarrassed the Royal York, the Bitoves, and, especially, my family. Fortunately, I discovered I was the luckiest man in the world to have a loving wife and a loving family who were so supportive throughout so many terrible days. And I had many friends who called or by other means sent me their regards and good wishes. John Haunts, who worked with me at the Royal York for many years, called to say he would pick me up to take me to my court dates. He was a great friend who was as good as his word. Canada's greatest criminal lawyer, Eddie Greenspan, let me know he believed in me. My own lawyer, Michael De Rubies, wouldn't take a cent from me for all his work on a case that dragged on and on. Even though the case was often written up in the papers, I was offered a number of high-profile jobs in the industry. I took on a couple of things, such as greeting people at the door of the Limelight Supper Club. Johnny Arena, who was in the process of preparing to sell Winston's, offered me the opportunity to run that legendary place for a time. During the trial, many wonderful people, especially the leaders of the Italian community, came to court on my behalf to testify to my character.

The early 1990's were the heyday of harassment and assault cases. Many people were wrongly charged and it wasn't unusual for the targets to commit suicide rather than be dragged through a court system seemingly more interested in witch-hunts than truth. The judge in my trial apparently decided that, because of my prominence, I should be made an example of since it was my word against hers. I was convicted, though the appeal court soon threw the conviction out. My exoneration was very satisfying, but the Crown attorney threatened he might re-try the case, holding out the possibility of another four years of heartache for me and my family. To avoid that, even if it was untrue, I was persuaded to plead guilty to a misdemeanor rather than a felony. It broke my heart to do it, and wish now I hadn't, but the grind of the wheels of "justice" was too much to bear. So, I put an end to the process. The toll would have been too great. I still don't understand what she thought she could get.

When it was over, a part of me thought I should just take life easier. After all, I was now 66 and I'd been working since I was five years old. But I felt I had to face the public. I wanted people to know that I could still look them in the eye and show them that I was alive and well. Somewhere in the back of my mind, an old dream that I'd put out of my head years earlier kept coming back to me.

I felt I had to have my own restaurant, a warm, even cozy Italian place where I could share my memories over good food with friends old and new. It wouldn't be a posh club for the powerful and privileged like some restaurants, such as Winston's, used to be. Those days were over. I wanted it to be like a small Imperial Room in feeling, but much more intimate. Many people thought I was nuts. Why open a restaurant? But I figured if God gave me the energy, for which I was very grateful, why not?

In February of 1994, at 66 years old, I opened Louis Jannetta's Place in a small hotel in downtown Toronto. With the help of Patti and a good designer, it had chandeliers and mirrors, low lighting, private banquettes with emerald velvet as well as tables, a large bar area, and about five hundred pictures on the wall of all the stars I had the pleasure of knowing. Many people said they felt like they were entering Sardi's in New York. Maybe my place had a New York style to it. I wasn't sure. It had been quite a while since I had dined out in New York.

The food was in the Italian tradition, but updated. My first chef was Carmelo Mantione, the son of the great Fredericko Mantione, one of Italy's finest chefs. He came up with wonderful fresh soups, eight pastas, six fish dishes, veal, chicken, generous servings of vegetables and potatoes, big steaks, grilled swordfish and salmon steaks.

I was very proud of the place. I thought of it as my home in terms of the warmth of the welcome and the attention I loved to lavish on my guests, some of whom I'd been serving since World War II. Even if they had to limp in, they still came by for special occasions. So did special guests, like Tony Bennett, who always dropped in when he was in town.

I enjoyed almost everything about the place -- speaking and singing and even cleaning tables. I took great pleasure, as I always had, in attending to people's needs and showing them the kind of hospitality that was becoming rare. As I had told my staff at the Royal York so often so many years before, I told my own staff of eighty-five, "Before you come to work every day, prepare for it as though you were about to attend a wedding."

During all the years it was up and running, whenever I phoned home, my wife was always at home alone. I was at the restaurant most days from noon till two or three in the morning and sometimes stayed overnight at the hotel rather than make the long way home. If Corinne had known what life would be like in the fifty years ahead, she would have never married me. It finally got to me, leaving me with a sick feeling in my stomach every day.

I sold the restaurant and, soon after, we sold our place in the country and our condo in Florida. But I've been so much happier in the past few years with so much less. I live for my family, for my children and grandchildren and even a great-grandchild. The Lord's been very good to me, despite some serious medical problems that are now happily in the past. Life has been very good, and remains so. Invitations to dinners and shows still flow in, as do invitations to talk shows on radio and TV.

Every six months or so, I meet with the food and beverage alumni of Toronto, all with top jobs in the city—at the Albany Club, York Club, Granite Club—all of whom learned a lot at the Royal York just like me. We trade stories of a great profession, looking after people and making them happy. It's something we can all be very proud of.

And even after these many years away from the Imperial Room, so many people still approach me on the street, in stores or hospitals or restaurants. They like to say hello and share their memories of an era of elegance that I treasure as much as they do, a magnificent exciting time of talent and grace that should never be forgotten.

999 JOE